Self-Sufficiency

›me Brewing

Self-Sufficiency

Home Brewing

John Parkes

NEW
HOLLAND

Published in 2009 by New Holland Publishers (UK) Ltd
London • Cape Town • Sydney • Auckland
www.newhollandpublishers.com

Garfield House	80 McKenzie Street	Unit 1	218 Lake Road
86–88 Edgware Rd	Cape Town 8001	66 Gibbes Street	Northcote
London W2 2EA	South Africa	Chatswood	Auckland
United Kingdom		NSW 2067	New Zealand
		Australia	

ISBN   978 184773 460 0

Senior Editor   Corinne Masciocchi
Design   Melissa Hobbs at e-Digital Design
Main illustrations   Michael Stones
All other artwork   e-Digital Design
Production   Laurence Poos
Editorial Direction   Rosemary Wilkinson

CONTENTS

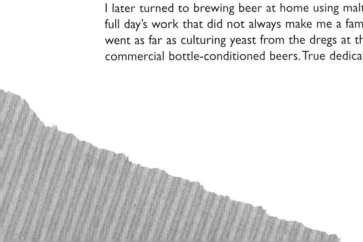

Over a period of thirty years, I have progressed from a home brewer brewing from kits to owning my own microbrewery, and every day I still learn something new about brewing.

My first job after leaving University was working for a large retail chemist in the chemical production department. Other factories on the same site manufactured home brew kits and some of my friends were fortunate enough to work in product development within these departments.

Purely in the cause of science, I would also help out the product development department by testing new recipes for the home brew kits. This involved brewing and then drinking the beer. Difficult as this task was, I carried on manfully and tested many recipes of every imaginable combination: those for bitter, stout and lager made with malt extract, with a combination of malt extract and grain, and using dried and liquid yeasts. I developed a taste for home brewing and a desire to brew beer that was like the stuff I drank in the pub.

I later turned to brewing beer at home using malted grains and hops – a full day's work that did not always make me a family favourite! I even went as far as culturing yeast from the dregs at the bottom of certain commercial bottle-conditioned beers. True dedication to the art!

No book can, in my opinion, claim to be the complete guide to brewing because it is an enormously complex subject that requires years of study to fully comprehend. I have spoken to several head brewers in large organizations who have left me dazed and confused with their elaborate explanations of the mashing and fermentation processes.

I have tried to offer brewing styles to suit as many people as possible. For those with little time but a keen desire to start home brewing, there is a chapter on brewing from kits. For those with more time, you can try to develop the craft by using either a combination of malt extract, grain and hops, or by really going back to basics and using just malt grains and hops. Some aspects of brewing are common to all of these styles, and these are described in the pages on brewing from kits, which those moving on to more advanced styles of brewing will be guided back to.

The chapter on cleanliness, in particular, should be read carefully before attempting any type of home brewing. Cleanliness is crucial to every form of home brewing, so ensure you always maintain a high standard of cleanliness across your brewing activities. No matter how much time and effort you put into brewing beer, putting it into a container that has not been sterilized correctly will result in it being ruined and all your efforts going to waste. I hope you will find the text easy to read and that this book will help you produce beers that you will enjoy both making and imbibing.

John Parkes

About beer

Beer has been around for thousands of years. Its diverse flavours and thirst-quenching properties make it one of the most popularly enjoyed alcoholic beverages. This chapter looks at the history of beer and the way in which its production has moved from the home to become a worldwide multi-million dollar industry.

Beer beginnings

Origins

Beer is quite possibly the world's oldest alcoholic beverage, dating back to at least the 6th millennium BC, and recorded in the written history of Ancient Egypt and Mesopotamia. Historians believe that beer was discovered by accident by the peoples of these regions. Barley was one of the staple grains of these parts, and it was soon discovered that if grain was allowed to get wet, germinate and then quickly dried off (a process known as malting), it would become sweeter and more suited for making breads and cakes.

It was a short leap from the discovery of malting to the discovery of beer. Probably quite by accident, someone allowed their malted barley to get wet and remain exposed to the elements. Naturally-occurring wild yeasts then contaminated this exposed liquid. Because malted barley contains sugars that are the perfect nutrition for yeast, the yeast took hold and multiplied, creating a bubbly soup of alcohol and malted barley by-products that eventually became the first beer. Once this process was discovered and refined, it became quite easy for the brewer to separate the beer from the spent yeast, which could then be cultured into the next batch of beer.

Chemical tests of ancient pottery jars reveal that beer was produced about 7000 years ago in what is today Iraq, making it one of the first ever recorded biological engineering tasks using the process of fermentation. In Mesopotamia, the oldest evidence of beer is believed to be in the form of a 4000-year-old Sumerian tablet depicting people drinking a beverage through reed straws from a communal bowl.

Beer became vital to all the grain-growing civilizations of Eurasian and North African antiquity, including Egypt. Knowledge of brewing was passed down to the Greeks, who in turn taught the Romans to brew. The Romans called their brew 'cerevisia', from Ceres, the Roman goddess of agriculture, and Latin for 'strength'.

Beer was very important to early Romans, but during the Roman Republic wine displaced beer as the preferred alcoholic beverage, and beer became a beverage considered fit only for barbarians. Tacitus, a senator of the Roman Empire, wrote disparagingly of the beer brewed by the Germanic peoples of his day. Thracians were also known to consume beer made from rye, ever since the 5th century BC, as the Greek historian Hellanicus of Lesbos records in his works.

Hops and beer

The use of hops in beer was written about in 822 by a Carolingian abbot and again in 1067 by Abbess Hildegard of Bingen, who wrote: 'If one intends to make beer from oats, it is prepared with hops.' The custom of flavouring beer with hops was known since the 9th century at least, but was only gradually adopted because of difficulties in establishing the right proportions of ingredients. Before that, a mix of various herbs known as 'gruit' had been used, but they did not boast the same conserving properties as hops. Beer flavoured without hops was often spoiled soon after preparation and could not travel very far. The only other alternative way to produce beer that would keep was to increase the alcohol content, but this was expensive.

By the 13th century, hopped beer was perfected in Germany and this longer-lasting beer, combined with standardized barrel sizes, allowed for large-scale export. The Germans also pioneered a new scale of operation and an increased level of professionalism. Previously, beer had been brewed at home, but the production was now successfully replaced by medium-sized operations of about eight to 10 people. This type of production spread to Holland in the 14th century and later to Flanders, Brabant, and finally reached England by the late 15th century.

Europe

Until medieval times, beer largely remained a homemaker's activity. The oldest operating commercial brewery is the Weihenstephan Abbey in Bavaria, which obtained the brewing rights from the nearby town of Freising in 1040. By the 14th and 15th centuries, beer making was gradually changing from a family-oriented activity to an artisan one, with pubs and monasteries brewing their own beer for mass consumption.

Hopped beer was imported to the English town of Winchester from the Netherlands as early as 1400, and by 1428 hops were being planted all over the country. The popularity of hops was at first mixed; the Brewers' Company of London went so far as to state:

'No hops, herbs, or other like thing be put into any ale or liquore wherof ale shall be made but only liquor (water), malt, and yeast.'

In 1516, William IV, Duke of Bavaria, adopted the Reinheitsgebot (the Bavarian Purity Law) which was perhaps the oldest food regulation in use throughout the 20th century. The Reinheitsgebot ordered that the ingredients of beer be restricted to water, barley and hops. Yeast was added to the list in 1857 after Louis Pasteur's findings on the role of yeast in the fermentation process. The Reinheitsgebot was officially repealed from German law in 1987.

Until recent times, most beers were top-fermented (fermented at relatively warm temperatures of around 20°C/68°F where the yeast rises to the surface). Bottom-fermented beers (beers fermented at cooler temperatures of around 8°C/46°F using a strain of yeast that ferments at the bottom of the beer) were discovered by accident in the 16th century, after beer was stored in cool caverns for long periods of time – a process now termed 'lagering'. Lagers have since largely outpaced top-fermented beers in terms of commercial production and worldwide consumption.

Asia

In Asia, there is pre-historic evidence that shows brewing began around 5400 BC in Sumer, southern Iraq. Some recent archaeological finds also show that Chinese villagers were brewing alcoholic drinks as far back as 7000 BC. Asia's first brewery was incorporated in 1855, although it was established in the late 1820s by Englishman Edward Dyer in the town of Kasauli in India under the name Dyer Breweries. The company still exists today and is known as Mohan Meakin, and comprises a large group of companies across many industries.

The Industrial Revolution

Following significant improvements in the efficiency of the steam engine in the mid-18th century, industrialization of beer became a reality. Further innovations in the brewing process came about with the introduction of the thermometer in 1760, closely followed by the hydrometer, a simple but invaluable instrument that allowed brewers to measure attenuation (a measure of how much sugar in the wort has been fermented into alcohol by the yeast).

The hydrometer transformed the brewing process of beer. Before its introduction, beers were brewed from a single malt: brown beers from brown malt, amber beers from amber malt, and pale beers from pale malt. With the help of the hydrometer, brewers were able to compare the yield from equal weights of different malts.

Brewers observed that pale malt, though more expensive, yielded around 50 per cent more fermentable extract per unit of weight than the cheaper brown and amber malts, making it more cost-effective. Once this fact was established, brewers switched to using mostly pale malt for all beer types, supplemented with a small quantity of highly-coloured malt to achieve the desired colour for darker beers.

All malt starts life as pale malt, and it is the kilning process that transforms both its colour and flavour. In general, none of these early malts were sufficiently shielded from the smoke involved in the kilning process, and consequently, early beers had a smoky component to their flavours. Evidence suggests that maltsters and brewers constantly tried to minimize the smokiness of their finished beer.

Writers of the period describe the distinctive taste derived from wood-smoked malts, and the almost universal revulsion it engendered. The smoked beers and ales of the West Country were famous for being undrinkable – locals and the desperate excepted. The following extract from *Directions for Brewing Malt Liquors* in 1700 goes some way to describing the general feeling:

> *'In most parts of the West, their malt is so stenched with the smoak of the wood, with which 'tis dryed, that no stranger can endure it, though the inhabitants, who are familiarized to it, can swallow it as the Hollanders do their thick black beer brewed with buck wheat.'*

The invention of the drum roaster in 1817 by Daniel Wheeler allowed for the creation of very dark, roasted malts that were free from the unpleasant smoky taint brought about by roasting over open fires. The externally-heated drum roaster was able to produce a range of dark malts suitable for contributing to the flavour of porters and stouts. The development of the drum roaster was prompted by a British law preventing the use of any ingredients other than malt and hops in beer; prior to this, colouring of beers had been achieved using alternative ingredients. Porter brewers, employing a predominantly pale malt grist, urgently needed a legal colourant, and Wheeler's patent malt was the solution.

Modern beer production

Prior to Prohibition in the 1920s and early 30s, there were thousands of breweries in the United States, mostly brewing heavier beers than modern US beer drinkers are used to. Most of these breweries went out of business, although some converted to producing soft drinks.

Bootlegged beer was often watered down to increase profits, beginning a trend, still ongoing today, of the American palate's preference for weaker beers. Consolidation of breweries and the application of industrial quality control standards have led to the mass-production and mass-marketing of light lagers.

The decades after World War II saw a huge consolidation of the American brewing industry: brewing companies would buy out their rivals solely for their customers and distribution systems, shutting down their brewing operations. Smaller breweries, including microbreweries or craft brewers and imports, have become more abundant since the mid 1980s. By 1997 there were more breweries operating in the United States than in all of Germany, historically the most established brewing nation.

Many European nations have unbroken brewing traditions dating back to the earliest historical records. Beer is an especially important drink in countries such as Belgium, Germany, Ireland and the United Kingdom, with nations such as France, the Scandinavian countries, the Czech Republic and many others having their own methods, history, characteristics and styles.

There is a significant market in Europe, and the United Kingdom in particular, for 'live' beers. These unfiltered, unpasteurized brews contain live yeast, and are awkward to look after because not only do they continue to ferment in the cask but there is also a risk of air getting into the cask, turning the beer sour. 'Dead' beers, on the other hand, are easier to look after. These are beers that have had all traces of yeast removed before being pasteurized and transferred into airtight metal casks. Live beer quality can suffer with poor care, but many people prefer the taste of a live beer to a dead one. While beer is usually matured for relatively short periods of times compared to wine – a few weeks to a few months – some of the stronger so-called real ales have been found to develop character and flavour over the course of as much as several decades.

In 1953, New Zealand brewing pioneer, Morton Coutts, successfully developed the technique of continuous fermentation, a process which involves beer flowing through sealed tanks, fermenting under pressure and never coming into contact with the atmosphere, even when bottled, thus eliminating the possibility of the alcohol oxidizing into acetic acid (vinegar) and spoiling the beer. Coutts went on to patent this process which is still in use today by many commercial brewers.

In comparison, Marston's Brewery in Burton-on-Trent, England, still uses open wooden Burton Union sets for fermentation in order to maintain the quality and flavour of its beers. Belgium's lambic brewers go so far as to expose their brews to outside air in order to pick up the natural wild yeasts which ferment the wort. Traditional brewing techniques protect the beer from oxidation by maintaining a carbon dioxide blanket over the wort as it ferments into beer.

Traditional brewing techniques are still widely used for the sake of maintaining the quality and uniqueness of the final product, which suffers if brewed using the more efficient industrial processes developed in modern times. Today, the brewing industry is a huge global business, consisting of several multinational companies and many thousands of smaller producers, ranging from brewpubs to regional breweries.

Advances in refrigeration, international and transcontinental shipping, marketing and commerce have resulted in an international marketplace, where the consumer is presented with hundreds of choices between various styles of local, regional, national and foreign beers.

Beer styles

The evolution of beer styles

The style of a beer is often indicative of the region of the world in which it was originally brewed. The factors affecting the style of beer produced include the quality of the water available, the range of locally-grown ingredients, notably cereal grains and hops, yeast strains and ambient temperature.

Certain towns within a country are well known for their water supply and the fine beers that are produced from this water; Burton on Trent, in England, is one of these places. Cereal crops vary from country to country, although most brewers around the world have used barley as the basis for their beers, giving rise to regional variations from the use of other malted grains and adjuncts.

Hops are a crucial ingredient in determining the style of a beer; the variety of hops grown in an area will greatly influence the taste and aroma of the beer made from those hops. The Bavarian region is renowned for its range of beers, and the floral hop flavours and aromas, particularly those attributed to the noble hop varieties, contribute to the style of beers brewed in that region. Eastern European regions and the south east of England, notably Kent, were also favoured hop growing areas, each with their distinctive varieties, which helped to determine the styles of beer brewed in the surrounding districts.

Yeast, particularly its fermentation characteristics, contributes much more to the flavour of a beer than is widely acknowledged. The naturally occurring yeast strain in a region affects the type of beer produced in that region; top-fermenting yeasts create different beers to bottom-fermenting yeasts. Before the advent of sophisticated temperature control systems the ambient temperature of a region would have determined how the beer was brewed. Colder climates would have tended to utilize yeasts which could operate at lower temperatures with longer fermentation times, resulting in beers with different flavours to those using top-fermenting yeasts.

Hops, along with alcohol content, contribute to the storage life of a beer; heavily hopped beers keep longer and are capable of travelling further than lightly hopped beers. The term IPA, which stands for India Pale Ale, refers to the strong, heavily hopped beers brewed in England which were sent out to the members of the military serving in India. This term is often misused by modern brewers who sometimes apply the title to low-gravity pale beers.

Taxation has also affected the type of beer brewed in a country, as high alcohol content beers often have attracted higher levels of duty, which is ultimately reflected in the price of the beer. This was particularly true in Ireland where the Guinness stout consumed there was of a lower alcohol content than the stout which was exported in order for it to be cheaper for local people to buy.

English beer styles

Being a country with a temperate climate, the United Kingdom has a wide variety of beers to suit the varying seasons. Many microbrewers and some of the larger brewers create seasonal beers at different times of the year.

Beer styles around the world vary immensely and are generally driven by the local climate and indigenous varieties of hops and grain. The style of brewing is also dependent on the ambient temperatures and the historical development in the regional brewing industries.

CAMRA, the Campaign for Real Ale, has been a driving force in reviving traditional beer in pubs in the UK, which has aided the revival of small independent breweries. Beers can be classified in the following categories:

Mild beer
Historically, mild has been a dark beer with a low alcohol content and low hopping levels. It was originally named because of its age, being a younger beer than the 'old ales' generally served.

There has been a rapid decline in mild sales in recent years, and many smaller breweries have attempted to revive an interest by varying the style of the beer, creating higher ABV (alcohol by volume) beers and also lighter coloured ones. Whether purists would accept that these beers fall into the mild category is perhaps a matter for debate.

Golden ales
Golden ales are pale and well hopped with strengths ranging from 3.5 to 5.3 per cent. They are usually dry on the palate with citrus hops overtones. They are best served cool.

Pale ale and IPA
First brewed in London and Burton-on-Trent for the colonial market, India Pale Ales were strong in alcohol and high in hops: the preservative character of the hops helped keep the beers in good condition during the long sea journeys.

Beers with less alcohol and hops were developed for the domestic market and were known as pale ale. Today, pale ale is often a bottled version of bitter, although many smaller breweries are reviving the traditional pale ale and IPA styles.

Light bitters
These are bitters that have an ABV of 3.4 per cent or lower and, like mild, have fallen into decline in recent years. They are often, but not always, also light in colour.

Bitter

Bitter is generally deep bronze to copper in colour due to the use of slightly darker malts, such as crystal, that give the beer fullness of palate. It has a higher hopping rate than mild and light bitters, and generally more body. It has an ABV of 3.4 to 3.9 per cent. Best bitter has the same characteristics of bitter in terms of colour and hopping rate but has an ABV in excess of 4 per cent. To achieve a higher ABV, the brewer must start off with a beer that contains more fermentable sugars than a weaker beer. The specific gravity of the beer before the yeast is added is called the 'original gravity', often termed OG. Generally speaking, the higher the OG, the stronger and often more full-bodied the finished beer. This is due to the increased presence of non-fermentable constituents in the wort, giving the beer a fuller mouth feel.

A further development of bitter comes in the shape of Extra or Special Strong Bitters, which have an ABV of 5 per cent or higher. These beers are often strongly flavoured and have a sweet finish, which can be something of an acquired taste.

Old ale

Old ale recalls the type of beer brewed before the Industrial Revolution, which was stored for months or even years in unlined wooden vessels known as tuns. The beer would pick up some lactic sourness as a result of wild yeasts, lactobacilli and tannins in the wood, adding a distinct flavour to the beer. Old ales do not have to be especially strong: they can be no more than 4 per cent alcohol although many current versions are considerably stronger than this. The hallmark of this style is that the ale undergoes a lengthy period of maturation, often in bottles rather than bulk vessels. Old ales typically range from 4 to 6.5 per cent ABV.

Barley wine
Despite the name, this is not a type of wine but rather a robust, often richly coloured ale. Barley wine is usually very strong, often with an ABV of between 10 and 12 per cent, and is stored for periods as long at 18 months or two years to mature and allow the complex flavours to mellow. It is traditionally served in 'nips' (approximately 200 ml / ⅓ pint measures).

Porters and stouts
Porters are complex in flavour, range from 4 to 6.5 per cent ABV and are typically black or dark brown; the darkness comes from the use of dark malts. Stouts use roasted malted barley to create the dark colour and add a distinguishing finish to the beer. Stouts can be dry or sweet and range from 4 to 8 per cent ABV.

Lager

Sadly, many of the beers that claim to be lagers do not do justice to the quality beers produced in the true lager-brewing areas of the world, notably Eastern Europe. To brew 'true' lager at home is almost impossible. Although you can buy very good quality lager yeasts and malts, the traditional 'lagering' process is beyond the reach of most home brewers. This doesn't mean that you can't have a try, of course. Your lager will probably taste better than the majority of the cold fizzy beers that are purveyed as lager!

Lager production process

The key difference between ale and lager is in fermentation; lager is fermented at a much lower temperature than ale and uses a different type of yeast.

The primary fermentation period for lager takes at least twice as long as for ale; this time is furthermore compounded by weeks or months of lagering. The term 'lagering' means the storage of beer for long periods of time in cool conditions; originally this would have been in caves, which was a common practice throughout the medieval period. Now, lager is stored in temperature-controlled fermentation and conditioning tanks.

As the low-temperature fermentation (which can take place at temperatures as cool as 0–5°C/32–41°F) allows diacetyl, a natural by-product of fermentation, to remain free in the fermenting beer, the fermentation temperature may briefly be raised near the end of the primary fermentation to allow the consumption of this chemical. This is called the diacetyl rest.

Before the introduction of refrigeration, this reliance on lower temperatures separated Europe into 'lager' and 'ale' spheres, with warmer countries generally producing ales and colder ones producing lagers. Difficulties in temperature control also create a disincentive for microbrewers to produce lagers because of the huge capital costs of the equipment required.

One exception to the rule of low-temperature lager brewing is found in a beer style known as steam beer, or California Common. The strain of yeast used in steam beer had originated in Germany and was brought over to

breweries in the central and eastern states of America. In the 1840s and 50s the same strain was used in breweries in California on the west coast. The higher ambient temperatures in that region caused brewers to favour shallower fermenters in order to better control fermentation; over several generations, evolutionary pressure led to the emergence of a lager strain which produced the best beer at temperatures of 18–20°C (64–68°F).

The choice of lager beer's grains and hops is, in principle, the same as for ale, despite the nomenclature 'lager malt' sometimes encountered in the United Kingdom.

The majority of lager in worldwide production is light in colour and usually represents the helles, pale lager or Pilsner styles. The flavour of these lighter lagers is usually mild and the producers often recommend that the beers be served refrigerated. However, the examples of lager beers produced worldwide vary greatly in flavour, colour and composition.

Most lagers are brewed in the continental style, originating in continental Europe, and consequently follow central european recipe formulations: the grist is composed mostly of Pilsner malt, Vienna malt or Munich malt, with caramel malts added to improve sweetness and head retention, and others added only for colour. The selection of hops is usually made from noble hops such as Saaz, Hallertau, Tettnanger, Strisselspalt or Lubelski.

Lagers often also feature large proportions of adjuncts, usually rice or corn. Adjuncts entered American brewing as a means of thinning out the body of American beers, balancing the large quantities of protein introduced by six-row barley. However, adjuncts are now often used in beer making to introduce a large quantity of sugar, and thereby increase ABV, at a lower price than a formulation using an all-malt grain bill.

In colour, helles and pale lager represent the lightest lagers; the darkest are Baltic porters. Darker German lagers are often referred to as dunkel lagers (dunkel meaning dark in German).

Commercial lager production

Modern methods of producing lager were pioneered in the early 19th century by brewers Gabriel Sedlmayr the Younger, who perfected dark brown lagers at the Spaten Brewery in Bavaria, and Austrian Anton Dreher, who began brewing a lager, probably of amber-red colour, in Vienna in 1840–41.

With improved modern yeast strains, most lager breweries use only short periods of cold storage, typically one to three weeks. Longer periods of storage would add hugely to the cost of lager production, although some commercial lagers are still marketed with the implication that they are matured in the 'old-fashioned' way.

In 1953, New Zealander Morton Coutts developed a process known as continuous fermentation (see opposite), which allowed the production of lager at a much faster pace, albeit with a reduction in flavour development. This development made possible the mass production of lager beer at a rate competitive with ales. As this technology was adopted worldwide, the light lager style emerged, quickly becoming the most popular style of beer in much of the industrialized world.

Since the 1950s, lager has displaced ale as the type of beer most consumed in the United Kingdom, and also constitutes the overwhelming majority of beer produced and sold in the United States, China, Japan, France, Italy, Russia and most, if not all, countries where beer is made and consumed.

The flavour of a lager can be quite simple, with the mildest being light lagers. Lagers with the most complex flavours are typically the darkest, although few lagers feature strong hop flavouring compared to ales of similar alcohol by volume. In general, however, lagers display less fruitiness and spiciness than ales, simply because the lower fermentation temperatures associated with lager brewing cause the yeast to produce fewer of the esters and phenols associated with those flavours. Lagers represent some of the world's most alcoholic beers. The very strongest lagers often fall into the German-originated doppelbock style, with the strongest of these, the commercially-produced Samichlaus, reaching an ABV of 14 per cent.

The continuous fermentation plant

The drawing below shows the workings of a continuous fermenter.
Wort is fed from the copper into the hold up vessel where a
quantity of recycled yeast is added; the fermenting beer flows
through the two continuous fermenting vessels at such a rate that
the fermentation is completed when the beer flows into the yeast
separator, where the yeast is separated from the beer. The yeast
then flows into the yeast washer and the beer into maturation
vessels (MVs). After washing with distilled water, some of the yeast
is added to the hold up vessel to keep the fermentation process
alive whilst the excess yeast (yeast reproduces during fermentation
so there is always an excess) is sold off to make products such as
yeast spreads. The carbon dioxide gas (CO_2) produced is collected,
compressed and then stored for sale. Efficiently it is sometimes
used to dispense the beer at the point of sale.

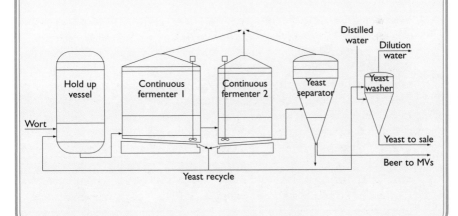

Ingredients

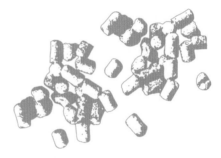

High quality beer is made from malted barley, hops, water and yeast. Sometimes other ingredients, called adjuncts, are added to give the beer particular characteristics. Like any other aspect of life, you only get out what you put in, so it is always advisable to use the best ingredients you can afford.

Water

Water is the main ingredient for brewing. Most beers are around 4 to 5 per cent alcohol, which means that they are 95 to 96 per cent water. Brewers always refer to the water they use as liquor, which can be confusing as water does not contain any alcohol!

Many of the world's most famous breweries owe their success to the water they use, often a naturally available local supply. Sometimes the water is drawn from a spring or well and its unique quality adds specific characteristics to the finished taste of the beer.

If you are lucky enough to have access to a spring or well, it is advisable to have the water tested by a recognized authority to check that it is suitable for drinking. It may be necessary to treat the water in some way. But in most cases you will probably be taking water directly from the kitchen tap. This water will have been treated by your water supplier and there will be a number of chemicals present. For your first attempt at brewing, I suggest using the water directly from the tap, unless it has a strong smell of chemicals when it is cold. If this is the case, boil the water to sterilize it and help drive off any dissolved chlorine before using.

You could contact your local water supplier to find out the level of hardness or softness of your water. Based on the findings of the report, you can buy water treatments to improve the quality of the water. Your local home brew shop will sell various water treatment materials that can be added to the water to make it more like the water used in breweries but these additives will not remove the chemicals that are already present. Alternatively, you can buy purified or distilled water to use as your brewing liquor although it will be lacking in any naturally occurring salts.

I recommend experimenting with a couple of brews, using water straight from the tap and then judging for yourself if it makes good beer. If it doesn't, then go ahead and try a water treatment.

Malt

Malt is produced when cereal grains are exposed to a process called 'malting'. The most commonly used grain is barley, although wheat malt is also available. At the end of the malting process, the resulting pale malt can be treated in kilns to add different levels of colour and flavour.

Other grains, such as wheat, may be malted, although the resulting malt may not contain enough enzymes to convert the starch present in the grain fully and efficiently; this means that it will not produce the sugars needed to give the beer its alcohol content. Non-barley malts are often used with a predominantly barley malt grist to increase the overall availability of enzymes.

The malting process

A maltings, sometimes called a malthouse or floor maltings, is typically a long, single-storey building in which the process of malting is carried out. For the purposes of this explanation, we will consider barley as the cereal to be malted. Barley is the most commonly malted grain, in part because of its high diastatic power, or enzyme content; this aids the conversion of starch to sugar in the mashing process. Barley also has a husk which not only protects the chit during malting but also forms a natural filter bed when the sweet liquor is run off the mash tun and sparging is taking place.

Barley used in the malting industry must meet special quality specifications with properties which lie within the brewer's specifications. The suitability of barley for converting into malt is determined by its variety, nitrogen and moisture content. Barley is analyzed by the maltings before the malting process is started.

The grains are steeped in water to start off the germination process. The barley absorbs water via the embryo, and after approximately 24 hours, a white 'chit', or root, appears. After the chit appears the grains are transferred to malting beds where germination is allowed to proceed; the speed of germination is controlled by temperature and aeration of the malt bed, while moisture content is maintained by spraying. The grain bed is turned either by hand or with a rotating screw to prevent grains sticking together.

After around five days the sprouted barley is spread on a perforated wooden floor which is heated to halt the germination. Original maltings used smoke, coming from an oasting fireplace via smoke channels, to heat the floor to around 55°C (131°F) and thus the sprouted grain. Malting is a combination of two processes: sprouting and kiln-drying.

In the 1940s, pneumatic plants began to replace traditional floor maltings. In these, large fans are used to blow air through the germinating grain beds and to pass hot air through the malt being kilned. All malting processes are batch processes, which means that one batch of grain has to be fully treated before a new batch can be started. Floor maltings will, depending on their size, have batch sizes of around 20 tonnes, whereas 100 tonnes is more usual in a pneumatic plant.

The process of malting develops the enzymes that are required
to convert the grain's starches into sugars; single molecule sugars
(saccharides) such as glucose and fructose, and double molecule sugars
(disaccharides) such as sucrose. It also develops other enzymes, which
break down the proteins in the grain into forms that can be converted
into alcohol by yeast.

After malting, the malt grain can be roasted to varying degrees
to produce malt grains with varying levels of sweetness and
colour. Pale malt, the natural product of malting, is sweet if
chewed but quite powdery in its consistency. It has a flavour
and aroma similar to the commercial beverage Ovaltine.
Crystal malt, by way of contrast, has been slightly roasted
and has a pronounced sweet, toffee-like flavour and a brown
colouration. A list of malts and their characteristics is provided
on pages 32–5.

The primary mash ingredient is malted barley grain. Home brewers
and commercial brewers generally use recipes that consist of a large
percentage of pale malt, which provides the majority of the sugar during
the mashing process and, subsequently, the alcohol in the finished beer.
The selection of malts, other grains and adjuncts in the mash is called the
grain bill or grist. The grist constituents of a beer determine the colour,
malt flavour and strength of the beer. Other flavours are added to the
beer from the selection of hops; this will be discussed later.

Smaller percentages of other types of malt are added to the grist
to impart degrees of colour and flavour. The general rule is that the
grist will contain no more than 10 per cent of malts and adjuncts other
than pale malt; that means that the grist will be at least 90 per cent pale
malt. Pale malt is termed 'base malt', whilst all other malts are called
specialty malts.

Types of malt

The list below provides information on the taste characteristics of various malts and some information relating to enzyme content, which is an indication of how much the malt will contribute to the activity in the mash tun during the mashing process.

Commercial brewers will buy whole grain and mill it to crush the grains. Milling will be finely controlled to provide exactly the correct level of crushing to suit the hydration and mashing equipment being used in the brewery. Small commercial brewers usually buy grain that has been milled (crushed) at the maltings because the maltings staff will have the expertise to crush each type of grain to the correct consistency.

It is not practical to malt or roast your own grain at home. Although it is possible to crush the grain yourself, I would advise buying grain which has already been crushed. If it's good enough for small commercial brewers then it's probably good enough for you! All the malts mentioned in this section are readily available from home brew shops or on the Internet.

Pale malt

Pale malt, as its name suggests, is light in colour and generally constitutes the majority of the grist in many styles of beer. The exception to this can be lager beers; these are brewed with a grist containing a large percentage of lager malt, although this term is sometimes a misnomer. Pale malt is dried at temperatures calculated to preserve all the brewing enzymes in the grain. The large volume of production and the fact that it requires little kilning make it the cheapest malt available. Pale malts are kilned at around 95–105°C (203–221°F).

Mild malt

This is often produced from the Triumph variety of barley, which is used extensively on the Continent for lager malt. Mild malt is kilned slightly hotter than pale malt to give a fuller flavour and a sweetness popular in mild beers.

Stout malt

As its name implies, stout malt is used for brewing stout beers. Although stouts are usually dark in colour, stout malt is quite pale. The colour of stouts comes from the addition of roasted malt and, often, roasted unmalted barley.

Amber malt

Amber malt is a more toasted form of pale malt, kilned at temperatures of 150–160°C (302–320°F). It is used in some English browns, milds and old ales to add colour and a distinctive, quite powerful, biscuit taste, so use it sparingly. Its low enzyme content means that it should be used in conjunction with other malts.

Brown malt

Brown malt is traditionally used in dark ales, and is kilned at high temperatures over a hardwood fire, which gives it a distinctive smoky flavour.

Chocolate malt

Chocolate malt is similar to black malt, but it is roasted for a shorter time and at a lower temperature. This means that it has a less harsh flavour, which is smoky rather than bitter. It is used in dark beers, often in conjunction with roasted unmalted barley. It has no enzymatic content.

Coffee malt

Coffee malt is lighter than chocolate malt and has, as its name suggests, a distinctive coffee aroma. One to use with care!

Black malt

This is similar to chocolate malt except that the malt is kilned to a much higher temperature. This high temperature destroys all the enzymes and some of the starch contained in the malt, leaving it with no enzymes and little fermentable extract. It has a bitter flavour and is used to add flavour and colour to dark beers.

Crystal malt

Undried malted barley is taken directly from the malting process and raised to around 65°C/149°F where it is held until the starch is converted to sugar. It is then kilned at about 250°C (482°F) which caramelizes the malt as it dries, leaving it a golden-red colour. The nutty, caramel flavour and residual sugars give the body and sweetness that are traditionally features of British bitter beers.

Peated malt

This malt has been treated by being smoked over a fire made from peat moss. It will provide a marked smoky, spicy aroma and flavour, and should be used in moderation as the flavour and aroma are very pronounced.

Pilsner malt

Pilsner malt is used on the Continent to produce lager beers and was developed in the 19th century. This malt is kilned slowly at a temperature of 50–60°C (122–140°F) to dry it before it is toasted at 80°C (176°F). The malt is a very pale colour with a strong, sweet flavour and has a very high enzyme content, which allows it to be used as a base malt. It has been adopted by many brewers as an addition to their pale beers because of its flavour and high yields.

Vienna malt

Vienna is an aromatic malt that is kilned at a higher temperature than Pilsner malt and so is somewhat darker. Because of this, it will add colour and flavour to beers brewed in the style of Vienna or Märzen beers. It can be used as a base malt because of its enzyme content.

Munich malt

Munich malt is darker and fuller-flavoured than Vienna malt. It can be used in dark and amber lagers and is an essential ingredient in German bock beers. It has a high enzyme content despite its high kilning temperature.

Rauchmalz

Rauchmalz is only produced in Bamberg, Germany, and is used to brew that town's world famous Rauchbier. The malt is kilned over open fires made of beech wood logs, giving it a smoky taste and aroma. It can also be used in beers such as brown ales and porters, adding an additional unusual flavour.

Acid malt

Acid malt is used for making high-class lagers. It contains lactic acid, which lowers the mash pH, producing the same effect as adding gypsum (calcium sulphate) to the brewing liquor but producing a softer palate than if gypsum is used. Adding gypsum to the brewing liquor is carried out to make the liquor similar to that which is available naturally in Burton upon Trent, England. This water is reputed to produce some of the best beers in the world.

Honey malt

Honey malt is similar to crystal malt but has a softer palate. It is highly kilned but in such a way that the roasted overtones associated with crystal malt are less noticeable. It is not commonly available.

Melanoidin malt

This is an aromatic malt from Bamberg, Germany, that has a full flavour and a colour slightly paler than crystal malt. It can be used in medium to dark beers, especially Munich-style lagers.

Any unmalted barley grain that is added to the grist is called an adjunct.

Adjuncts

Adjuncts are any grains that are used in the grist which are not
a form of malted barley. These include unmalted barley, wheat,
sorghum, millet, rice and corn.

Unmalted barley

Roasted barley

This is unmalted barley, which has been heavily
roasted to produce a very dark grain.
It has a slightly bitter burnt taste which
is popular in stouts but it can also be
used in small amounts to add colour
and a distinctive crisp, burnt finish to
bitter and dark beers.

Black barley

Black barley is roasted to a higher degree
than roasted barley, producing a darker colour
and a pronounced burnt flavour. The flavour is very
strong and the grain should be used sparingly.

Flaked barley

Flaked barley is a versatile adjunct produced by simply rolling the raw
grain. It imparts a grainy flavour and can be used in quite large quantities
in bitters and dark beers, although it can cause haze problems in paler
beers. As well as adding a distinctive flavour it helps with head retention.

Torrefied barley

Torrefied barley is made from barley kernels that have been heated until
they pop like popcorn. It adds a distinctive flavour to the beer and helps
with head retention.

Wheat

Wheat malt
Wheat has no husk and is therefore difficult to malt and cannot form a natural filter bed during the mashing and sparging process. It is used to make German weiss bier and can make up 50 per cent of the grist for a home brewer. It also helps with head formation and retention.

Torrefied wheat
Torrefied wheat is used to aid head retention, producing a firm, creamy head on the beer. It adds little in the way of flavour and has no fermentable content.

Wheat flour
Wheat flour was used in early brewing days in the same way as torrefied wheat is used today, to improve head retention. Torrified wheat was not available at that time. It was mistakenly cast into fermenting beer to aid the yeast in the belief that it was yeast food.

Rye

Beers made with rye have a very distinctive spicy, dry flavour, probably the best known being the German Roggenbier. Historically, the use of rye to make beer was forbidden; it was only allowed to be used in bread-making. Rye, like wheat, has no husk and is therefore difficult to malt and does not form a natural filter bed in the mash tun. It must be used with other grains that will provide the filter bed.

Sorghum and millet

Sorghum and millet are gluten-free grains often used in African brewing, sorghum malt being rarely available outside certain African countries. The dark, hazy beers made with these grains are suitable for people who are allergic to gluten. Millet is used in the Indian alcoholic beverages *chhaang* and *pomba* whilst both sorghum and millet are used together in the Namibian drink *oshikundu*.

Rice and corn

Flaked rice and corn are the perfect substitutes for any recipe calling for the addition of sugar. They are virtually flavourless but provide some body without darkening the colour and also assist in clearing. Commercial breweries utilize these adjuncts in place of malt or sugar as a way of adding strength to the beer at low cost as they are both readily available and cheaper. Flaked rice is used in Asian countries to produce products such as sake and makkoli.

American beers, in particular, are brewed with malted six-row barley, which is high in protein. Most European beers are brewed with two-row barley, which means that there are two rows of grains on the head as opposed to six rows on the head of six-row barley. Corn was originally introduced into the brewing of American beers to help to 'thin out' the beer by adding additional sugar, and therefore alcohol, but no 'body'. This style of brewing developed over time to produce the pale lager style of beer which is now synonymous with America and other 'new' lager producing countries; 'new' as opposed to the German and eastern European lager styles.

Corn, like rice, is generally used in a flaked form, where the grain is rolled and must be combined with malts that have a high enzyme content to allow the mash to perform effectively.

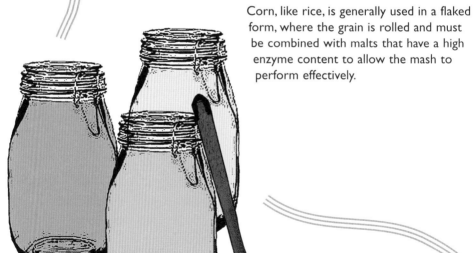

Non-grain solids

Buckwheat and quinoa, while not grains, both contain high levels of starch and protein, and no gluten. Therefore, some breweries use these plants in the production of beer suitable for people with coeliac disease, either on their own or in combination with sorghum.

Syrups and extracts

Sugar, other than that which is produced from the grist in the mash tun, can be added to the copper – hence the term 'copper sugar'. As well as refined white sugar, there are many other sources of sugar available, from raw cane to honey. The problem with some of these is that they can add a very distinctive flavour to the beer, sometimes in an overpowering way, so it is advisable to use them carefully. One English brewer even had an image of a bee on the beer label to indicate that there was honey in the beer. Most beers that taste of 'honey' will gain that flavour from a combination of the malt and hops used in the brewing process.

DME, diastatic malt extract, is an exception to this rule as it is produced by evaporating the sweet liquor from a fully converted mash until a syrupy liquid is produced. DME is commonly used in home brewing as a substitute for base malt.

Regional differences

Britain
There are numerous breweries in Britain, many of which are very small, like mine. The brewers pride themselves on producing distinctive beers, often a range of them, with seasonal specials, which is probably due to the British obsession with seasons and the weather! Base pale malt is

produced from low-nitrogen barley; the most popular variety used to be Maris Otter but this has been overtaken in recent times by other varieties such as Halcyon, Pipkin, Chariot, Fanfare and Westminster.

Improvements in the control of the kilning process during the industrial revolution lead to the development of a range of malts and removed the smoky aftertaste common to earlier malts. The availability of this range of quality malts has allowed the industry to develop along very individual lines. Historically, beer was brewed and drunk in a very small geographical area, often with a brewery in each town or village; the increase in the number of micro-breweries in recent years has seen a huge revival in the availability of local beers in free public houses.

Continental Europe
Similarly to Britain, the drying of malted grains over open fires imparted a distinctive flavour to the beers that were produced from these grains. Some aspects of this remain in Germany with the continuing production of Rauchmalz, which is the German term for smoked malt. Beech is often used as the wood for the fire, which gives the malt its flavour; it is used as the primary component of Rauchbier. Malt smoked over alder wood fires is used in Alaskan smoked porters.

The caramel malts used in central Europe are made in a similar way to British crystal malt where the grain is moistened and heated at temperatures of around 55–65 °C (131–149°F) in a rotating drum to convert the starch to sugar before being heated to higher temperatures for browning. This produces a dark grain which is sweet. Caramel malts are produced in a range of colours by kilning at higher temperatures for varying periods of time.

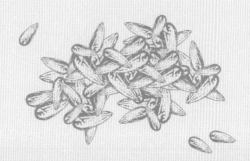

The United States

Brewing in America has absorbed and adapted the brewing techniques of both Britain and Europe and uses the malts available in these regions. As already mentioned, American brewing tends to utilize the six-row varieties of barley which are high in protein and produce a full-bodied beer which is often 'thinned out' with the use of adjuncts such as corn and rice flakes. Another malt commonly used in America is Victory malt, which is lightly roasted and imparts a biscuity, caramel flavour to the beer.

Hops

General information

Hops are the female flower cones of the hop plant known as *Humulus lupulus*. The hop plant is a vigorous climbing herbaceous perennial, usually grown up strings in a hop field, hop garden or hop yard. Many different varieties of hops are grown by farmers all around the world, with different types used for particular styles of beer.

They are grown in two ways, depending on the variety. The tall varieties are grown along wires that are stretched between poles at a height of around 3.5 to 4 metres (11 ft 4 in to 13 ft); the hedge varieties are grown along a similar pole and wire arrangement but to a height of around 2 metres (6 ft 5 in).

Hops are used primarily as a flavouring and stabilizing agent in beer, as well as in other beverages and in herbal medicine. The first documented use of hops in beer dates back to the 11th century.

Hops contain several characteristics that are favourable to beer. They balance the sweetness of the malt with bitterness, contribute flowery, citrus, fruity or herbal aromas, and have an antibiotic effect that favours the activity of brewer's yeast over less desirable microorganisms.

The first documented instance of hop cultivation was in 736, in the Hallertau region of present-day Germany, although the first mention of the use of hops in brewing in that country was 1079. Not until the 13th century in Germany did hops begin to start threatening the use of fruit for flavouring.

In Britain, hopped beer was first imported from Holland around 1400; however, hops were initially condemned in 1519 as a 'wicked and pernicious weed'. In 1471, Norwich banned the plant from use in the brewing of beer, and it wasn't until 1524 that hops were first grown in southeast England. It was a further century before hop cultivation began in the United States in 1629.

World production

As of 2005, the ten leading countries for hop cultivation (based on reported total production) were:

COUNTRY	OUTPUT (TONNES)
Germany	34,438
USA	23,494
China	10,576
Czech Republic	7,831
Poland	3,414
Slovenia	2,539
United Kingdom	1,693
Spain	1,537
Ukraine	1,474
France	1,372

(Source: International Hop Growers Convention: Economic Commission Summary Report 2001–06)

Important production centres are the Hallertau Valley in Germany, which, in 2006, had more hop-growing area than any other country in the world, and the Yakima (Washington) and Willamette (Oregon) valleys in the United States. The principal production centres in the UK are in Kent, which produces Kent Goldings hops, and Worcestershire.

Global prices and availability of hops vary from year to year depending on the weather and subsequent yields of the different varieties.

Until mechanization, the need for massed labour at harvest time meant hop-growing had a big social impact. For instance, many of those hop picking in Kent, a hop region first mechanized in the 1960s, were Eastenders. For them, the annual migration meant not just money in the family pocket, but a welcome break from the grime and smoke of London. Whole families would come down on special trains and live in hoppers' huts and gradients for most of September, even the smallest children helping in the fields.

Sonoma County in California was, pre-mechanization, a major US producer of hops. As in other hop-growing regions, the labour-intensive harvesting work involved large numbers of migrant workers travelling from other parts of the state or elsewhere for the annual hop harvest.

During the Great Depression of the 1930s, many workers were migrant labourers from Oklahoma and the surrounding region who had recently come to California. Others included locals, particularly older school children. Sometimes whole families would work in the harvest.

The remnants of this significant hop industry are still noticeable in the form of old hop kilns that survive in Sonoma County. In part because of the hop industry's importance to the county, local Florian Dauenhauer of Santa Rosa, the seat of Sonoma County, created one of the earliest and most significant hop-harvesting machines but ironically this mechanization helped destroy the local industry. It enabled large-scale mechanized production which then moved to larger farms in other areas.

Hop processing

Hops have to be dried in an oast house before they can be used in the brewing process. Hop resins are composed of two main acids: alpha and beta acids. Alpha acids have a mild antibiotic and bacteriostatic effect, and favour the exclusive activity of brewing yeast in the fermentation of beer. Beta acids do not isomerize during the boil of wort, which means that they retain their aroma characteristics during the boiling process, and so have a negligible effect on beer flavour. Instead they contribute to beer's bitter aroma, and high beta acid hop varieties are often added at the end of the wort boil for aroma. Beta acids may oxidize into compounds that can give beer off-flavours of rotten vegetables or cooked corn.

The flavour imparted by hops varies by type and use. Hops boiled with beer are known as 'bittering hops' and produce bitterness; hops added to beer later impart some degree of hop flavour if they are added during the final 10 minutes of boil, or hop aroma if they are added during the final 3 minutes, or less, of boil. Hops added at the end of the boil are generally known as aroma hops. Adding hops after the beer has fermented is known as 'dry hopping'; these hops add aroma, but no bitterness.

The degree of bitterness imparted by hops depends on the degree to which otherwise insoluble alpha acids are isomerized during the boil, and the impact of a given amount of hops is specified in International Bitterness Units. Unboiled hops are only mildly bitter. Flavours and aromas are described appreciatively using terms that include grassy, floral, citrus, spicy, piney and earthy.

Most common commercial lagers have fairly low hop influence, while true Pilsners should have noticeable noble hop aroma, and certain ales, particularly the highly-hopped style known as India Pale Ale, or IPA, can have high levels of bitterness.

Hop varieties

Particular hop varieties are often associated with beer styles. For example, pale lagers are usually brewed with European, often Czech or German, hop varieties such as Saaz, Hallertau and Bobek. English ales commonly use hop varieties such as Fuggle, Golding and Bullion, although the new generation of brewers have expanded the use of new hop types. North American varieties include Cascade, Columbia, Willamette and Amarillo. Many of the recently introduced hops, such as Cascade, have very distinctive aromas and are used predominantly for this reason.

Noble hops

The term 'noble' is a traditional designation for hops grown in Southern Germany. The varieties took the name of the town or region in which they were predominantly grown. For instance, Tettnanger originated in a small town in Southern Germany called Tettnang. The four varieties are Hallertauer Mittelfrüh, Tettnanger, Spalter and Saaz. Saaz was also known by its original Czechoslovakian name, Zatec, before political reform moved the location of the growing region. Hops, like grapes, are affected by the climatic conditions in which they are grown and so each hop variety would have flavours and aromas unique to the growing region. Officially the term 'noble hops' can only be applied to these four varieties when they are grown in their original location.

Within the brewing fraternity, Fuggle and East Kent Goldings are sometimes referred to as noble hops and although they share many characteristics with the four true noble hops, they are not actually noble hops.

Noble hops are traditionally low in bitterness and high in aroma, and are therefore well suited to the production of the light Eastern European beers such as the classic Pilsner Urquell, often considered to be one of the world's finest lager beers.

Noble hop types
Hallertau or *Hallertauer*
A delicate aroma hop used mainly in lager type beers and some of the lighter English cask-conditioned ales. It is grown in the Hallertau, Spalt, Hersbruck, Tettnang and Baden-Bitburg-Rheinpfalz areas of Germany. Hallertauer Mittelfrüher is the traditional Hallertau variety although its acreage is gradually decreasing due to disease and has been replaced by Hersbrucker. (Alpha acid 3.5–5.5 per cent.)

Saaz
Saaz hops are traditionally used for European lager type beers, but are used in other light beers, giving an earthy lager hop flavour found in the Czech beers such as Pilsner Urquell. The variety has developed over many years from hops grown in and around the Zatec area. (Alpha acid 3–4.5 per cent.)

Spalt
Spalt is the newest of the Hallertau type aroma hops in the classic style with a delicate, spicy aroma. It was bred in Germany and released for cultivation in the late 1980s. It is grown in the Hallertau and Spalt areas of Germany and in the USA. (Alpha acid 4–5 per cent.)

Tettnang
Tettnang is a traditional aroma hop which is used in European lager type beers. It is grown mainly in the Tettnang cultivation area of Baden-Bitburg-Rheinpfalz region of Southern Germany and also in the Hallertau region. (Alpha acid 3.5–5.5 per cent.)

Other hop varieties

Admiral
Admiral was bred in the UK to increase the range of its high alpha varieties. It is comparable to Target, but with a softer bitterness, and has a very pleasant hoppy character. (Alpha acid 13.5–16 per cent.)

Ahtanum
This is very distinctive hop from the USA with aromatic properties and moderate bittering. Its name is derived from the area near Yakima where the first Yakima Chief Ranches hop farm was established in 1869 by Charles Carpenter. (Alpha acid 5.7–6.3 per cent.)

Amarillo
Amarillo has a unique combination of floral and spicy aromas with good bittering quality. It was developed by Virgil Gamache Farms in the late 20th century. (Alpha acid 8–11 per cent.)

Apollo
Apollo has a high percentage of alpha acids and excellent resistance to disease. It was cultivated at Golden Gate Roza Hop Ranches in Prosser, Washington. (Alpha acid 20–21 per cent.)

Bramling Cross
Bramling Cross has a distinctive strong spicy/blackcurrant flavour and good alpha characteristics. It was bred in 1927 from a cross between Bramling and a male seedling of the Manitoban wild hop. (Alpha acid 5–7 per cent.)

Brewers Gold
Brewers Gold was developed from a breeding programme around 1917 by Professor Salmon in England. It gives interesting fruity and spicy characteristics to cask ales. (Alpha acid 7.1–11.3 per cent.)

Cascade
Cascade is an aroma variety that was developed in Oregon in the early 1970s. It is a cross between Fuggle and the Russian Serebrianker variety. It has a unique floral/spicy aroma and is very popular with some brewers due to the unique character imparted to the finished beer. (Alpha acid 4.5–6 per cent.)

Centennial
Centennial is a cross between Brewers Gold and a selected USDA male. It has floral qualities similar to that of Cascade and Chinook. (Alpha acid 9.5–11.5 per cent.)

Challenger
Challenger was bred from the Northern Brewer and Northdown strains. As a bittering hop it provides a refreshing, full-bodied, rounded bitterness, and as an aroma hop, a crisp, fruity character. (Alpha acid 5–9 per cent.)

Chinook
Released in 1985, Chinook adds strong grapefruit character to the beer. It was developed from a cross between a Petham Golding and a US selected male with high alpha acids. (Alpha acid 12–14 per cent.)

Cluster
Cluster has a well-balanced bittering effect and a deep fruity aroma. It is thought to be the result of a cross between an English variety and an American male hop. It is also known as Golden Cluster, being used as the sole bittering hop in the Queensland, Australia beer XXXX Gold and XXXX Bitter. (Alpha acid 5.5–8.5 per cent.)

Columbus
Columbus, Tomahawk and Zeus were produced at the same time and have similar very high alpha properties. Columbus and Tomahawk have since been proven to be the same strain. (Alpha acid 14–17 per cent.)

Crystal
Crystal is an aromatic and fruity aroma hop released for commercial production in 1993. It was bred from Hallertauer Mittelfrüher and a male mildew-resistant aroma hop, USDA 21381 M. (Alpha acid 3.5–5.5 per cent.)

Eroica
A strongly-flavoured bittering hop used in wheat beers. (Alpha acid 9–12 per cent.)

First Gold
First Gold has good aroma and bittering qualities, producing a well-balanced bitterness and a fruity, slightly spicy flavour. It is a dwarf hop bred from a cross-pollination of WGV with a dwarf male. The aroma is similar to Goldings but it has a higher alpha content than traditional aroma hops. (Alpha acid 6.5–8.5 per cent.)

Fuggle
Probably the most famous traditional English aroma variety, Fuggle is also grown in Slovenia as Styrian Goldings and the USA as Oregon Fuggle. It gives a grassy, slightly floral aroma and produces a clean, refreshing, full-bodied flavour. (Alpha acid 4–5.5 per cent.)

Galena
Galena has a strong blackcurrant aroma similar to that of the Bullion variety. It is a cross from Brewers Gold developed in Idaho in the late 1970s. It has a moderate bitterness despite its high alpha content. (Alpha acid 12–14 per cent.)

Glacier
This is a new variety descended from Fuggle. It has a soft, fruity character with hints of apricot and pear. (Alpha acid 5.5 per cent.)

Goldings
This is possibly the quintessential traditional English aroma variety. It has a delicate, smooth, slightly spicy aroma that produces the classic Goldings finish. Goldings have been grown in England for over 100 years and were named after the grower who developed them. They are known as East Kent Goldings if grown in East Kent, Kent Goldings if grown in mid-Kent, and Goldings if grown elsewhere, such as the USA. (Alpha acid 4–5.5 per cent.)

Herald
Herald is a dwarf high alpha variety which has been successfully used as a substitute for Target where Target is found to have too harsh a bitterness. It produces a well-rounded, gentle citrus grapefruit flavour. This hop is a sister to Pioneer. (Alpha acid 11–13 per cent.)

Hersbrucker
Hersbrucker is a delicate aroma hop, with aromas of grass and hay, originally used in lager type beers as a replacement for the noble hop Saaz. It originates from the Hersbruck region of Southern Germany and is also grown in the Hallertau area and the Spalt region. (Alpha acid 3–5.5 per cent.)

Horizon
Horizon is a high alpha aroma hop bred from a cross made in 1970 between the male plant 64035M and the female plant USDA 65009, which is also the parent of Nugget. It has good aromatic and bittering properties, giving a soft, bitter finish. (Alpha acid 11–13 per cent.)

Liberty
Liberty is a relatively new American aroma hop and is similar to the Hallertauer Mittlefrüh. It also has many similarities to a Goldings hop with just a hint of citrus lemon flavour. It originates from a cross made in 1983 and was released as a variety in 1991. (Alpha acid 3–5 per cent.)

Lublin
Lublin, or Lubelski, has a flavour somewhere between Styrian Goldings and Saaz with a grassy, hay-like aroma. It has a harsher bitterness than the noble varieties. (Alpha acid 3–5 per cent.)

Magnum
Magnum is a dual-purpose hop which was bred in 1980 at Hüll, the German Hop Research Institute, from the American variety Galena and the German male 75/5/3. (Alpha acid: 10–12.6 per cent.)

Millennium
Millennium is a replacement for the variety Nugget and provides an alternative to the varieties collectively known as Columbus, Tomahawk and Zeus. It is grown in Washington and Oregon. (Alpha acid 15.5 per cent.)

Mount Hood
Mount Hood is an aroma variety that was developed in Oregon in the late 1980s from a cross between Hallertauer Mittlefrüh and an aroma type male. It has similar characteristics to the Hallertauer Mittlefrüh and Hersbrucker varieties with a mild herbal aroma. (Alpha acid 5–8 per cent.)

Nelson Sauvin
Nelson Sauvin is a new variety, which was developed in New Zealand. The flavours of fresh gooseberries are reminiscent of those produced by the sauvignon grape, hence the name. (Alpha acid 12–14 per cent.)

Newport
This hop was developed around 1996 and released in 2002. It has a high alpha acid content and a resinous pine flavour. (Alpha acid 10–17 per cent.)

Northdown
Northdown was released by Wye College in 1970 and is a seedling of Northern Brewer; it is also related to Challenger and Target. It has good alpha acid, an excellent flavour and a soft aroma. (Alpha acid 7.5–9.5 per cent.)

Northern Brewer
Northern Brewer was developed in England from a cross between Brewers Gold and Canterbury Golding and its direct descendant is Northdown. It is a dual-purpose variety which gives excellent bittering properties and a pleasant aroma. (Alpha acid 8–10 per cent.)

Nugget
Nugget is a cross between Brewers Gold and a high alpha male which was released in 1982. It is popular in the USA and has a herbal, spicy aroma. (Alpha acid 12–14 per cent.)

Pacific Gem
Pacific Gem is a high alpha hop from New Zealand with a pleasant aroma and useful bitterness. It has a distinctive berry fruit aroma and 'woody' flavour. (Alpha acid 14–16 per cent.)

Palisade
Palisade is a variety developed from Tettnang which is similar to Willamette. It has good alpha acid for an aroma hop and is useful in IPAs and beers that require high alpha acid combined with good aroma. (Alpha acid 6–10 per cent.)

Perle
Perle was bred at the Hop Research Institute in Hüll, Germany, and is an excellent floral and spicy aroma hop, similar to Hallertauer Mittlefrüh but with a higher alpha acid content. (Alpha acid 7–9.5 per cent.)

Pioneer
Pioneer is a dual-purpose hop that is related to the English Herald and distantly related to Wye Yeoman. It has a citrus lemon aroma and a moderately high alpha acid content. (Alpha acid 8–10 per cent.)

Polnischer Lublin
Polnischer Lublin is a finishing hop which is widely believed to be a clone of Saaz, with a mild aroma similar to Czech Saaz and Tettnang. (Alpha acid 3–4.5 per cent.)

Pride of Ringwood
Pride of Ringwood became famous in 1965 when it was introduced as the highest alpha acid hop in the world. It is grown in Australia and used extensively in that country's pale ales and lagers, including the brand whose name is represented by a lot of Xs. (Alpha acid 7–10 per cent.)

Progress
Progress was developed at Wye college as a replacement for Fuggle, which had become susceptible to wilt, to which Progress is resistant. It has similar characteristics to Fuggle but is slightly sweeter with a softer bitterness. (Alpha acid 5–7 per cent.)

Santiam
Santiam was released by USDA in 1998 and was the result of crossing German Tettnanger, a selected triploid male and Hallertauer Mittlefrüh. It is a floral aroma hop with mid-range alpha acid. It gets its name from the Santiam River in Oregon. (Alpha acid 5–7 per cent.)

Sapphire
Sapphire has been bred to replace the Hallertauer Mittlefrüh variety, which has become susceptible to disease. It has a sweet, clean, citrus aroma with a hint of tangerine. (Alpha acid 2–4.5 per cent.)

Satus
Satus is used for its bittering and aromatic qualities and is similar to Galena. (Alpha acid 12.5–14 per cent.)

Select
Also known as Spalt Select, it is an aroma type which was bred in Germany and released for cultivation in the late 1980s. It is grown in the Hallertau and Spalt areas of Germany, and in the USA in Washington State. (Alpha acid 4–6 per cent.)

Simcoe
One of many varieties developed at Yakima Chief Ranches; it has a high alpha acid and was released in 2000. Simcoe hops impart a distinctive passion fruit flavour and aroma. (Alpha acid 12–14 per cent.)

Sterling
Sterling is an interesting cross-bred hop with Saaz, Cascade, Brewers Gold and Early Green featuring in the parentage. It is a floral hop with good alpha acid content. (Alpha acid 6–9 per cent.)

Strisselspalt
This hop is grown in the Alsace in France and is used mostly as an aroma hop in pale lagers. It has characteristics which are similar to Hersbrucker. (Alpha acid 3–5 per cent.)

Styrian Goldings
This hop is known in Slovenia as the Savinja Golding, although is the same as the English Fuggle, and was fully adopted by Slovenia in 1930 when their other varieties were exterminated by powdery mildew. The change in the political structure of Eastern Europe has resulted in the loss of the generic term 'Styrian', which has been replaced by the individual name of the hop. One of the popular varieties is Bobek. (Alpha acid 4.5–6 per cent.)

Summit
Summit is a dwarf hop variety grown in the Yakima Valley. It has a citrus, grapefruit flavour and can be used for bittering and dry hopping. (Alpha acid 17–19 per cent.)

Tardif de Bourgogne
Tardif de Bourgogne is a French aroma hop used predominantly in continental lagers. (Alpha acid 3.1–5.5 per cent.)

Target
Target was released from the Wye College breeding programme in 1972 as the first wilt-tolerant high alpha variety. It provides bitterness but is too harsh for aroma purposes. (Alpha acid 9.5–12.5 per cent.)

Tradition
A relatively new hop which was bred in 1991 from Hallertauer Mittlefrüh by the Hüll Hop Research Institute in Germany. It has grassy aromas, like Hallertau, but is easier to grow. (Alpha acid 5–7 per cent.)

Ultra
Ultra is the half-sister to Mount Hood, Liberty and Crystal. Its parentage includes Hallertauer Mittlefrüh and Saaz and it was developed in 1983, although not released for commercial production until March 1995. (Alpha acid 4.5–5 per cent.)

Vanguard
Vanguard is yet another cross developed from Hallertauer Mittlefrüh with similar characteristics. (Alpha acid 5.5–6 per cent.)

Warrior
Warrior is another of the Yakima Chief Ranches products, being a high alpha bittering hop. (Alpha acid 15–17 per cent.)

Willamette
Willamette is an aroma hop of the Fuggle variety developed in Oregon in the early 1970s. It has a blackcurrant and herbal aroma that is pleasant but quite strong. It takes its name from the Willamette Valley, an important hop-growing area. (Alpha acid 4–6 per cent.)

Making beer

This chapter will guide you through the various brewing processes, explaining the three most commonly used techniques available to the home brewer. Beginners may wish to start by brewing from a kit whereas more advanced brewers can follow the tried-and-tested recipes or experiment using their own blend of ingredients.

Cleanliness

This does not refer to personal hygiene, although a basic standard of this is generally a good thing to have in all aspects of your life! It is essential to keep all brewing equipment not merely clean, but sterile. This means that the equipment used to make beer and all containers used to store the finished beer, be they barrels or bottles, must be free of bacteria.

Sterilizing your equipment

You can buy proprietary sterilizing powder from your local home brew shop or online, and you should follow the instructions on the container carefully. It is also important to thoroughly rinse all equipment to remove any traces of the sterilizing solution prior to it coming into contact with the beer.

The easiest way to remember to sterilize all your brewing equipment is to do it before you do anything else. Ideally, you should have a spare bucket to hand for this purpose which should be readily available at all times; failing that, you can make up a solution of sterilizing solution in your fermenting bin.

Put all the equipment you are planning to use into the sterilizing solution and leave it to soak for at least the minimum length of time recommended by the manufacturer. Before using each item make sure you rinse it in clean water first to remove all traces of the solution. If you can arrange to work in an area that has a worktop, clean the surface with an antibacterial wipe or some sterilizing solution before placing any equipment on it. If the space isn't available, sterilize the lid of your fermenting bin and use it to rest your equipment on when it's not being used.

Sterilizing barrels

You can choose to store your finished beer in either a large barrel or a number of bottles, or a combination of both.

If you are using a barrel, check that it is clean and free from any residues from a previous brew. Use a bottlebrush with a long handle to clean any debris from the inside of the barrel.

If the residues are stubborn and will not shift easily, leave them to soak overnight in a dilute bleach solution. Use 2 teaspoons of household bleach to every 5 litres (1 gallon) of hot tap water. Alternatively you can use a sodium hypochlorite solution, which can be bought in various forms, such as baby equipment sterilizer or swimming pool sterilizer. Always follow the manufacturer's instructions with any proprietary products.

Put the lid onto the barrel and gently swirl the bleach/cleaning solution around so that all surfaces, including the lid, are completely wetted. Leave the barrel for a couple of hours, then gently swirl the cleaning solution around again. When the solution is cool, remove the lid and drain the barrel. Do not look into the barrel when it is full of cleaning solution as some may splash into your eyes (wear protective eyewear if you like). Rinse the barrel with cold tap water and inspect the inside for residues. Should there still be traces of dirt, repeat the overnight soaking and use a long bottle brush to remove the stubborn dirt. When all the residues have been removed, rinse the barrel again thoroughly with clean water before adding the sterilizing solution, which should be left in the barrel for the minimum amount of time recommended by the manufacturer before rinsing out.

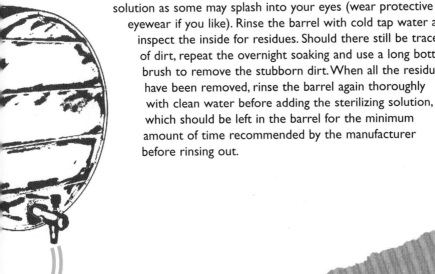

Sterilizing bottles

You can buy new 500 ml (18 fl oz) glass beer bottles from your local home brew shop or you could buy a selection of your favourite bottled beers, drink them and save the bottles. It is not advisable to use plastic bottles for home brewing as the pressure that builds up inside them may make them burst; this is not only dangerous but is also a terrible waste of good beer! Screw-top glass bottles seem to be quite a rare commodity these days but if you can find them, they are ideal for home brewing.

Using 500 ml (18 fl oz) glass bottles that have been crown capped by the original brewer will mean that they will also have to be crown capped when you are bottling your own beer. This means you will need to invest in a crown capper and a selection of crown caps. There is something immensely satisfying about taking the crown cap off a bottle of your own home-brewed beer and hearing that gentle hiss as the seal is broken; it is well worth all the effort of putting them on!

Whichever bottles you decide to use it is vitally important that they are scrupulously clean and sterilized before you transfer your finished beer into them.

Assuming you have opted for bottles that used to contain either beer from a previous brew or beer from a brewery, these bottles will contain dregs of beer that may well have started to turn sour (alcohol turns into vinegar as it is exposed to air). They will also have labels which you may want to remove. The easiest way to deal with these two problems is to soak the bottles in hot water.

Fill a bucket with hot water. I would recommend that you do not use your fermenting bin for this purpose because there is a possibility, however remote, that you could introduce unwanted infection by scratching the surface of the bin; it is better to use a bucket which will not later be used in the brewing process. Empty the dregs from the bottles into the sink or drain, rinse the inside of the bottles with clean, cold tap water, then immerse them in the water in the bucket and leave them to soak for an hour or so. After this time, the labels should simply peel off and any solid residues left in the bottles will rinse out. Use a bottlebrush to loosen any remaining solids. Rinse the bottles thoroughly in clean running water and then sterilize them in the sterilizing solution. Finally, thoroughly drain all the sterilizing solution from the bottles and rinse them in clean, cold tap water. They are now ready to transfer your finished beer into.

Do not use your fermenting bin to soak the bottles in hot water; use a clean, spare bucket instead.

Basic equipment

The equipment listed on these pages is all you need to brew beer from a kit. Many home brew shops sell a complete 'starter set' containing all the requisite items. Some additional equipment will be required for the more involved methods of brewing and these are listed later.

Plastic 25-litre (5½-gallon) lidded fermenting bin: this is the ideal size for the home brewer as most commercially-produced kits are geared up to make this volume, and you can produce a quantity that can be consumed in a reasonable amount of time. It is important that the bin be made from food-grade plastic to avoid it giving off any unwanted flavours, or worse still, colour entering the beer from inferior plastic. All fermenting bins supplied by reputable home brew stockists will be of an acceptable quality.

Thermometer: this should be made of glass and must not contain any mercury. The range should read from 0–110°C (32–230°F).

Hydrometer: this is used for measuring the specific gravity of beer, which helps you work out how strong the beer will be and when it is ready for putting into bottles or a barrel. You will need one which reads from 1010 to 1100. It is also useful to have a hydrometer jar that can hold the beer you are testing. All readings taken with a hydrometer must be at 20°C (68°F). If the wort or beer is not at this temperature, use the chart on pages 118–19 to correct the reading.

> **Science stuff**
> *Everyone knows that a thermometer measures temperature. A hydrometer's function is to measure the specific gravity of a solution, which indicates how much of a solid is dissolved in that solution. In the case of brewing, the hydrometer measures the amount of fermentable sugar which will eventually turn into alcohol so the hydrometer tells you how strong your finished beer will be. It will also indicate when most of the sugar has been turned into alcohol and it is time to 'rack' your beer.*

Sterilizing powder or solution: there are many proprietary sterilizing powders and solutions on the market. Take advice from your home brew shop owner and always carefully read the manufacturer's instructions.

Plastic stirrer: a long-handled plastic stirrer or spoon is essential, particularly when you are stirring hot liquids. Ensure that it is made from food-grade plastic.

Bottle brush: you will need this to clean the inside of bottles or barrels. Buy a long-handled brush so that you can reach into the murky corners of a 25-litre (5½-gallon) barrel.

Siphon tube: this is used for transferring the beer from the fermenting bin to either bottles or a barrel. It should be made of clear, food-grade plastic and be long enough to reach from the bottom of the fermenting bin to the bottom of the barrel or bottles when they are in the bottling position. It is a good idea to purchase a tap which fits onto the end of the tube so that you can control the flow if necessary. You can also buy a U-shaped piece of plastic or glass to fit onto the other end of the tube to prevent solids on the bottom of the bin from being sucked up the tube.

Separate sterilizing bin: not essential, but it is very handy to have a spare 25-litre (5½-gallon) bin that can be filled with sterilizing solution into which you can drop washed equipment. It is also useful for soaking bottles in if you are trying to remove old labels.

Ladle or large spoon: this should have a long handle (around 40–45 cm / 16–18 in) and be made of food-grade plastic or stainless steel.

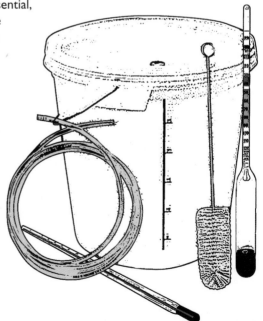

Home brewing methods

The process of making beer can be as straightforward or as involved as you want it to be. There are three ways to make beer:

From a kit

By far the simplest way to make beer, home brew kits contain all the ingredients you need in a concentrated form. If you just want to produce an alcoholic beverage that tastes fine and will not involve too much effort, then this option will suit your needs. Turn to pages 66–70 for more details.

Using malt extract, hops and adjuncts

The next step up is using malt extract as a base and then adding your choice of additional malt grains, adjuncts and hops. If you want to create a beer that suits your palate and have already tried, but not enjoyed, beer made from kits, then this could be the option for you. It is more time consuming and slightly more messy than the first option, but you should be able to produce a better quality, more individual beer. If this appeals to you, refer to Brewing from malt extract, hops and adjuncts on pages 76–82.

In the traditional way

This option is for those of you who are serious about making beer. Here, you start with crushed malt grains to produce the fermentable sugars and then add other malt grains, adjuncts and hops of your choice. If you have a passion for beer and are prepared to dedicate a serious amount of time, effort and, initially, money, then this is the option for you. After some practice you will be able to make beers to your exact requirements that will taste as good as, and arguably better than, many commercial brands. See Brewing the traditional way on pages 91–108.

Each of the three methods is presented as a self-contained guide. If you decide that brewing from kits is not for you and would like to progress to a more advanced form of brewing, go straight to the relevant pages. Whichever way you choose to make your beer, you will be able to produce it for a fraction of the price charged in most stores, bars, restaurants and pubs.

There are three common elements to all brewing styles which have already been covered but whose importance cannot be stressed enough:

- The first is cleanliness (see pages 58–61). It is important that you read this section carefully before you even begin brewing as it could mean the difference between your homemade beer tasting like beer and it tasting like vinegar! The equipment you use must be scrupulously clean at all times. Follow the instructions for sterilizing and rinsing to ensure that your equipment and storage containers are free from bacteria.

- The second common element is water. Water is the main ingredient in beer. There is always much discussion as to which type of water makes the best beer: hard water is often recommended for bitters, whilst soft water is supposed to be better for stout-type beers. Start by using water straight from the kitchen tap, unless you have access to a more natural potable supply, and see if this makes good beer. See page 28 for information on how to treat your water supply.

- The third is storage. Beer can be stored in barrels or other large containers. Beer stored this way tends to be less carbonated (fizzy) than beer stored in bottles. Bottled beers keep longer and exhibit slightly different characteristics when poured. See pages 71–3 for more on this.

Brewing from kits

The easiest way to brew beer is undoubtedly from a tin of concentrated wort. Many years ago, when I worked for a large company of chemists, 'beer kits' were available in three styles – bitter, stout and lager – these being the vague categories of beer available in pubs at the time.

Nowadays there is a plethora of beers available in kit form, some made by breweries and maltsters. Others are made by specialist companies that have spent many years refining their products. For more about maltsters and malt varieties see pages 29–34.

Your local home brew shop will stock its favoured range and the Internet has a bewildering array of beer and lager kits of all styles. I will use the term 'kit' throughout this section to refer to anything that contains a can of concentrated wort or for ingredients which do not involve carrying out any aspect of the brewing process other than adding boiling water to a can of concentrated wort. Wort is the brewing term for the mixture of sweet, malted barley sugar and the oils extracted from the hops that give the beer bitterness, flavour and aroma.

Most kits contain all the ingredients you need, including yeast, to make your brew. To produce a beer with more 'body', buy a kit that requires no additional sugar; the beer will be more akin to that produced by commercial real ale brewers. Many of my home brewing friends add sugar to their kits, regardless of the instructions, but this creates a 'thin' beer, which is too strong to drink in any quantity without the obvious after effects.

Basic beer kit brewing techniques

Select and purchase a suitable beer kit

Beer kits can be bought from your local home brew shop or on the Internet. If you choose to do the latter, you will be so overwhelmed with sites to choose from that you will probably be keener to find your local home brew shop instead!

I have presumed that, if you are making beer, you know what sort of beer you like and will choose a style that suits your palate, based on the manufacturer's description. The contents of the can will be concentrated malt extract mixed with hop extract. Some kits are made from real brewer's wort, which has been concentrated to produce a syrupy liquid.

Read and follow the instructions that come with the kit

It is important to follow the instructions closely to achieve optimum results. Any deviation may have disastrous results. Whatever the instructions state, do remember to sterilize and rinse all the equipment you are using before embarking on the brewing process.

Making the beer

The basic procedure for brewing beer from a can of concentrated wort is as follows:

1) Scrub clean and sterilize your 25-litre (5½-gallon) fermenting bin. Rinse it thoroughly with cold tap water.

2) Open the can of malt extract and stand it in a pan or bowl of hot water so that the level of water is about three-quarters of the way up the can. This will make the malt extract less viscous and easier to pour. Tip the contents of the can into

Tip
Stand the can of concentrated wort in a container of hot tap water for 15 minutes; this will make it easier to pour the contents from the can.

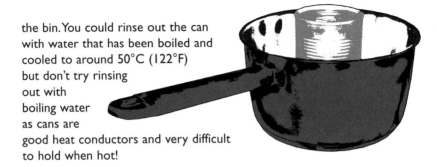

the bin. You could rinse out the can with water that has been boiled and cooled to around 50°C (122°F) but don't try rinsing out with boiling water as cans are good heat conductors and very difficult to hold when hot!

3) Add boiling water to the fermenting bin as instructed and stir until the contents of the can have dissolved – this is your wort.

4) Add cold tap water until the required volume is almost reached. Check the temperature: it should range between 18–25°C (64–77°F). Add more hot or cold water to achieve the required volume in this temperature range. It is important to maintain this temperature to allow the yeast to work effectively. Too cold and the yeast will not start the fermentation of the beer; too hot and it will die.

5) Add the yeast to the wort, closely following the manufacturer's instructions; this will usually involve mixing the yeast with sugar or about 250 ml (9 fl oz) of wort in a sterilized and rinsed container before adding it to the wort in the fermenting bin. This may not be in the instructions, but give the wort in the bin a good rousing with the plastic stirrer to introduce oxygen into the wort. Yeast needs oxygen to start working on the sugars in the wort and vigorous stirring will do just that.

6) Loosely cover the fermenting bin with its sterilized and rinsed plastic lid and put it in a warm place (20°C/68°F). If you are brave, just put it in a clean, warm place, free of dust and insects, with the lid off. Instead of a lid, you could use a clean cloth large enough to cover the bin but make sure it does not come into contact with the beer. <u>Do not</u> cover the bin tightly as this will starve the yeast of air which may cause problems with the fermentation and give rise to 'off' smells.

Science stuff
• *Yeast is the most underrated ingredient in brewing. It not only changes the sugar present in the wort at the start of the brewing process into alcohol by the end of it, but also affects the flavour of the finished beer. It is important to look after the yeast by keeping the wort at the correct temperature (between 18–25°C/64–77°F) both at the start of and throughout the fermentation process.*

• *Fermentation is the term that describes the process by which yeast converts the sugar in the wort into alcohol and carbon dioxide – the gas that makes beer fizzy.*

7) After a day or so, the top of the wort will be covered with a frothy mass flecked with brown, or simply just a brown layer – different yeasts work in different ways but as long as something is happening, you're on track.

8) Check the temperature of the beer with your (sterilized and rinsed) thermometer. It should be between 18–25°C (64–77°F). Now that there is some alcohol in the solution it is called beer instead of wort.

9) After three or four days, use your (sterilized and rinsed) hydrometer to see how the beer is progressing. Refer to the instructions supplied with it to check the specific gravity of the beer. Many hydrometers feature coloured bands that indicate when the beer is ready to be transferred into bottles or a barrel, but when the reading on the hydrometer reaches 1010, or thereabouts, your beer is ready to be transferred from the bin into your choice of storage container(s).

10) Add any finings that have been supplied with the kit according to the manufacturer's instructions. Finings come in powder or liquid form and help the beer to clear. Some finings are added to the fermenting bin, while others to the barrel or bottles.

Well, that's it! You should have now produced some thirst-quenching beer for a fraction of the price it would have cost you in a bar or supermarket. If you would like to customize the flavour of your beer you might like to try other kits or, better still, read on.

Science stuff
• *The carbon dioxide produced during the fermentation process acts as a protective blanket over the beer, effectively keeping air out.*

• *Although air, or the oxygen in it, was necessary at the start of the fermentation process, it is an unwelcome guest at the end. The alcohol in the finished beer reacts with the oxygen in the air to produce acetic acid, more commonly known as vinegar. This process is known as oxidation.*

Kit beer's shelf life

Beer made from a kit will keep in an unopened bottle for about six months for a weak beer with an ABV of less than 4 per cent. Stronger beers (over 5 per cent ABV) will keep for a year or more. Beer stored in barrels does not keep for as long, as air will inevitably enter the barrel as the beer is drawn off. Some barrels can be fitted with carbon dioxide-based pressure systems which are intended to make the beer last longer by filling the void created above the beer in the barrel as it is drawn off with a blanket of carbon dioxide, thus preventing the ingress of air. Air oxidizes the alcohol in the beer into acetic acid, commonly known as vinegar.

Transferring the beer into bottles or a barrel

It is advisable to skim off any yeast that is on the surface of the beer using a (sterilized and rinsed) ladle or large spoon before you begin to 'rack' it. (Racking is a brewing term which means transferring beer into your chosen storage container(s).) This prevents the yeast from being inadvertently sucked into the barrel or bottles.

Move the bin to a suitable location that will allow you to transfer the beer from it into your chosen container(s) with the aid of a siphon. To prevent the beer from spilling when you move it, put the lid firmly on the fermenting bin – 25 litres (5½ gallons) of beer is quite heavy and not easy to lift! Place the bin on a suitably strong surface, such as a kitchen worktop or table, at such a height that the beer will flow by gravity into your barrel or bottles. Ideally, the bottom of the bin should be about 30 cm (12 in) above the top of your barrel or bottles. It is very important that the area you are working in is clean and dust-free to prevent anything getting into the finished beer which may spoil it after all your hard work! It is advisable to move the bin a couple of hours before you start racking to allow any solids in the beer to settle to the bottom of the bin.

There are many good siphons on the market but I recommend choosing one that has a U-tube arrangement at one end so that the sediment, which will be lying on the bottom of the fermenting bin, does not get sucked into the barrel or bottles. It is also useful to have a tap fitted at the other end of the siphon so that you can better control the flow of beer into the barrel or bottles.

Start the flow of beer by immersing the U-tube into the bin, opening the tap, and sucking on the end of the tap – this allows you to cunningly sample the beer at the same time! Close the tap once the flow has started and then position it to allow the barrel or bottles to be filled when it is reopened. It is useful to have a glass or jug available to catch the initial flow as you close the tap, otherwise you may have a flood of beer on the floor.

> **Science stuff**
> *Liquids will only flow downhill, which is why rivers run down mountains to the sea and not the other way around. This is due to the effect of gravity. When you are siphoning your beer, the end of the siphon tube going into the barrel or bottles must be lower than the end that is in the fermenting bin, otherwise the beer will not flow. The higher the fermenting bin is above the barrel or bottles, the faster the beer will flow.*

Add sugar to the barrel or bottles according to the kit manufacturer's instructions. <u>Do not</u> add too much sugar as this could produce too much gas in the barrel or bottle, resulting in either the beer frothing everywhere when it is being poured or, worse still, the bottle exploding. This is potentially dangerous and a waste of good beer (see Science stuff, opposite).

However, if you do choose to add sugar to 'prime' your bottles, use about half a teaspoon to every 500 ml (18 fl oz) of beer. Adding sugar provides food for the small amount of yeast which is left in the beer and a secondary fermentation starts in the bottle. This produces carbon dioxide gas (CO_2), which is useful in small quantities as it gives the beer a sparkle after a week or so. However, if you add too much sugar, too much CO_2 will be produced, and there is a possibility that there will be either a geyser-like erruption when the bottle is opened or, worse still, the bottle may explode.

Leave about 2.5 cm (1 in) of space at the top of the bottles when you are filling them. When all the bottles are filled to the correct level, apply the crown caps. Follow the manufacturer's instructions when using your crown capping device and make sure that the caps are firmly fixed in place.

Science stuff

As an alternative to adding sugar to your barrel or bottles of beer, you could simply bottle it and wait for a couple of weeks. There will usually be some residual sugar in a finished beer and leaving it in a barrel or bottles for a couple of weeks allows a secondary fermentation to take place. Because the container is sealed, the carbon dioxide produced in the fermentation process makes the beer naturally fizzy. The brewing term for this is 'conditioned'.

When all the bottles have been capped and the barrel filled, place the beer in a warm place (around 20°C/68°F) for a week to get the secondary fermentation going and then move it somewhere cooler for a couple of days, such as a cellar or cupboard, where the temperature is around 12–15°C (53–59°F). Yeast will be produced during the secondary fermentation and this will settle more quickly to the bottom of the barrel or bottles if the beer is in a cool place.

Drinking your beer

After a week or so, sample the beer. The secondary fermentation, which has taken place during that time, will have made the beer fizzy and will also have produced a small amount of yeast. If you have bottled your beer, you will be able to see a thin layer of sediment on the bottom of the bottle; try not to disturb this when you pour the beer from the bottle into your glass.

If the beer is too 'flat' (not fizzy), move it back to a warm place for another few days and then try it again. If it is too 'lively' (fizzy), try chilling it before you pour it. If your beer is in a barrel, you may find that it gushes out for the first few glasses and then gradually slows down; this is because the pressure of gas inside the barrel reduces as the beer is poured (or 'drawn off' as brewers term it). The instructions that came with the barrel should explain how to overcome this.

Pouring your beer

Now you can start drinking the fruits of your labour! If the beer is bottled, it is important to pour it correctly:

- Have a glass ready that can hold all the contents of the bottle and open the bottle.

- Tilt the glass and then pour the beer gently down the side of the glass. It's important that the glass and bottle be angled correctly and that the pouring be done in a single movement, as the yeast sediment will be disturbed if you allow the beer to 'backwash' into the bottle by tipping it upright.

- When the bottle is almost empty watch for the yeast sediment following the beer and stop pouring before the yeast gets into the glass. Although the yeast will not harm you, it affects the flavour of the beer and will make it appear cloudy, which can put people off drinking it!

If you have stored your beer in a barrel, you will need to follow the manufacturer's instructions for dispensing the beer. Many beer barrels are called 'pressure barrels' because they have to be strong enough to withstand the pressure which builds up inside them during the secondary fermentation. Often you will find that the first few glasses come gushing out of the barrel and then the flow subsides.

To keep your beer tasting its best, never allow air to be sucked back up through the tap as you are pouring it as this will make the beer start to deteriorate. Some barrels have injection systems to maintain the pressure inside the barrel; consult the manufacturer's instructions for further detail.

It is easier to pour the beer and leave behind the sediment if you chill it slightly first. If the weather is cold, stand the bottle outside for half an hour. Alternatively, stand it upright in the fridge.

Brewing from malt extract, hops and adjuncts

Making beer using your own ingredients is a more challenging and
satisfying process than making beer from a kit. It is, however, slightly
messier and more time-consuming.

Equipment

In addition to the basic equipment listed on pages 62–3, you will also need
the following:

Large pan or similar: this can be made of aluminium or stainless steel;
cast iron is not really suitable, mainly because it is heavy. The pan should
be able to hold around 10 litres (2¼ gallons) of liquid, and should have
two sturdy handles, one at either side of the pan, so that it can be handled
safely when the contents are close to boiling point. This pan will be used
for boiling the malt extract, malt grain, adjuncts (if there are any) and hops
together.

Large sieve or filter bag: used for straining hops and grain. Ideally you
should use the largest rigid sieve or colander you can find, preferably made
from stainless steel. If you are using a colander, choose one with holes
that will not allow the grain to pass through. Plastic sieves are not ideal
because they lack strength. Plastic filter bags are available
from home brew shops, but they can be messy to
use and difficult to support, particularly when full of
wet grain.

Weighing scales: these should have a capacity to weigh up
to a minimum of 2 kg (4 lb 6 oz) with an accuracy to the
nearest gram. Digital scales are more accurate and easier
to use than mechanical ones.

Ingredients

The basic ingredients for any beer are water, malt and hops. In this section, I will explain about the different types of malt extract and hops that are available. A more detailed list of hop types can be found on pages 46–55.

Other ingredients can also be added to give the beer particular characteristics; these are called adjuncts and they will be covered later.

Malt extract

Malt extract can be bought from your local home brew shop or online. It is available in dried or liquid forms. The dried form is easier to handle and can be weighed accurately, but some argue that the liquid has a more realistic flavour; you will have to be the judge of that.

It is worth asking your home brew shop owner which malt they recommend, as most are keen, and often experienced, brewers themselves. They are usually very willing to offer advice if you ask them.

Malt gives strength and body to beer, whereas sugar will only provide strength and has a tendency to make the beer taste 'thin'. Beer brewed solely with malt will have a far superior flavour and body than beer brewed with a mixture of malt and sugar. The slight extra expense is well worth the investment.

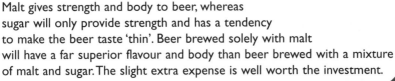

There are several different types of malt extract:

Extra light adds the minimum of colour for brewing lager and pale beers.

Light adds body and richness, and is especially useful when brewing lagers and pale beers.

Medium gives a rich malt flavour and the colour associated with traditional bitter.

Dark adds body, a dark brown colour and the flavour associated with dark beers such as stout, porter or brown ale.

Extra dark will add an almost black tinge to the beer, as well as flavour and body.

Wheat is made from a blend of 55 per cent wheat malt and 45 per cent barley malt. This is used in specialist beers and can also be added in small quantities to any beer to improve head retention.

Malted grains

Some malted grains do not have to be mashed to extract their sugar; crystal malt is one of these, which is why it has been chosen for the Traditional bitter ale recipe on pages 84–7. Your home brew shop will tell you which grains are suitable for this type of home brewing.

Hops

Hops are a relatively recent addition to beer but have become a major player in the way beer styles have changed. Hops serve three purposes:

• They add bitterness to the beer to balance the body given by the malt.

• They give the beer a pleasant aroma.

• They act as a preservative.

The latter use has diminished in importance over the years as the methods of storing and transporting beer have improved. Heavily hopped beers, such as India Pale Ale, were made using lots of hops which acted as a preservative on the long journey to India and other colonial outposts that hadn't yet mastered the art of brewing.

There are many varieties of hops, available from all over the world. Refer to pages 46–55 for a comprehensive list, which describes the different characteristics of each hop.

Hops come whole, as pellets or in the form of a liquid extract. Whole hops do not keep as well as pellets because they lose their aroma relatively quickly. Pellets tend to give a superior flavour and aroma and can be bought in small quantities that can be used all at once. However, pellets cannot be used alone in commercial brewing because whole hops are needed in the copper where they act as a natural filter bed when the beer is transferred from the copper to fermentation vessels. Pellets are often used in conjunction with whole hops.

Hops are added to the wort, the mixture of malt and water, in two stages. Bittering hops are added at the start of the boil to add bitterness to the beer; aroma hops, which are added at the end of the boil, give a pleasant aroma and taste.

Some hops are classed as 'dual purpose' and can be used for either bittering or aroma. Many hops can be used this way; it depends on your personal preference.

Hop types vary in popularity depending on which part of the world the beer is brewed in. Indigenous hop varieties often determine the characteristics of a region's beer.

Listed here are a few of the hop varieties I have used over the last couple of years while I have been brewing commercially. Most of these hops are now available through home brew shops. However, hops are cropped annually and sometimes become unavailable if the harvest of a particular variety has been poor. They generally become available again at the start of the next season. Further details of these hops can be found on pages 46–55.

Goldings: used in pale beers and bitters, both as bittering and aroma hops.

Cascade and Cluster: used in pale beers and bitters, both as bittering and aroma hops, but with the emphasis on aroma.

Bobek: these used to be one of a group of hops called Styrian Goldings but this name was dropped and renamed after the region in which the hops are grown. Good aroma or second hop.

Northern Brewer: used mainly as a bittering hop because it does not have a strong aroma.

Willamette: I used these as a substitute for Cluster when they are unavailable, but I have since moved on to Cascade because they have similar characteristics.

Hersbrucker: a traditional variety with good to very good aroma but sometimes rather low bitter content. It is considered a successor of Hallertauer Mittelfrüh and has a good tolerance to disease.

Adjuncts

Adjuncts are unmalted grains, such as corn, rice, rye, oats, barley and wheat used in brewing beer which supplement the main mash ingredients (usually malted barley) sometimes with the intention of cutting costs and sometimes to create an additional feature, such as better head retention.

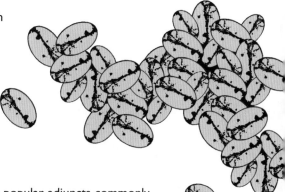

Listed here are some of the more popular adjuncts commonly used at this more advanced level of brewing expertise.

Flaked barley: adds body and aids head retention. It can cause a haze if used excessively in pale beers, but is a useful addition to stout-type beers.

Flaked maize: should be used sparingly as it imparts a corn-like taste to the beer; it helps finished beer to clear.

Flaked rice: adds strength without flavour and helps the finished beer to clear.

Roasted barley: this type of barley has been kilned for a long time and it has a strong, almost burnt, flavour. It is often used in stout-type beers but can be used sparingly to darken other beers and to add a distinctive flavour.

Torrefied wheat: this is used in any type of beer to improve head retention without affecting the flavour.

Finings

Finings are clearing agents used to help beer to clear. Without finings most beers would appear slightly cloudy, which isn't pleasing to the eye. Finings help fine, suspended solid particles stick together and fall out of the beer. This produces a clear beer and a layer of solids on the bottom of the container. There are three types of finings:

Copper finings are added to the pan of boiling liquor 5 to 15 minutes before the heat is turned off at the end of the boiling process. Follow the manufacturer's instructions.

Primary finings are usually added to the fermenting bin at the end of the fermentation.

Secondary finings such as Isinglass, or similar, are added to the finished beer in the barrel and sometimes in the bottle. Use them according to the manufacturer's instructions.

Science stuff

In simple terms, finings work by making the short chain proteins produced during the mashing and boiling stages of the brewing process stick together and form protein chains that are large enough to sink to the bottom of the fermenting bin, barrel or bottles. Finings added to the copper are called copper finings; those added to the fermenting bin are usually called primary finings; and those added to a barrel or bottles are called secondary finings. Many bottled beers do not have added secondary finings.

Recording the brewing process

Brewing is similar to cooking; you need to know what you want the finished product to taste like and you need a suitable recipe that will produce that taste.

The recipes featured on the next few pages have either been developed by myself or have been given to me by eminent home brewers.

It is useful to keep a record of what you do during the brewing process. There is nothing more frustrating than producing a master beer and not being able to remember how you made it.

I recommend you create a brewing record sheet stating the following information. Alternatively, photocopy the template on page 117.

- The name of the brew.
- The date and time you began the brew.
- The exact weight of each ingredient.
- The length of time you boiled the hops with the malt liquor.
- How long you left the hops to soak.
- The gravity of the wort before the yeast was added.
- The temperature of the wort when you added the yeast.
- Daily readings of temperature and specific gravity.
- Details of when you racked the beer and the containers, barrel or bottles used. It is also useful to label all the containers with the brew type and the date of filling.

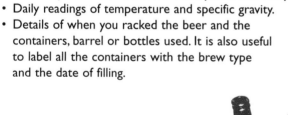

The process detailed here is a general guide for brewing beers using malt extract, crushed malt and hops. You may want to modify the way you do things as you become more experienced and develop your own methods.

~ Traditional bitter ale ~

It has been a long time since I brewed using ingredients other than grain, so I asked a friend of mine who runs a home brew shop to advise me on a suitable recipe, and this is one he came up with. It makes 25 litres (5½ gallons) of a strong bitter beer that is not too heavy. These are general guidelines for the production of any beer using a combination of malt extract, other grains and adjuncts which do not require mashing. This recipe does not use any adjuncts, just a combination of liquid and dried malt extract combined with crushed crystal malt. The process remains the same if you choose to add adjuncts to the ingredients.

Malt
3 kg (6 lb 10 oz) pale liquid malt extract
1 kg (2 lb 3 oz) medium dried malt extract
250 g (9 oz) crushed crystal malt

Bittering hops
50 g (2 oz) First Gold hops
25 g (1oz) Bramling Cross hops

Aroma hops
50 g (2 oz) East Kent Goldings hops

You will also need
Copper finings
Packet of dried beer yeast large enough for 25 litres (5½ gallons)
or 50–60 g (2 oz) wet brewer's yeast
Finings for the fermenting bin
Finings for the barrel or bottles

1) Open the can of malt extract and stand it in a pan or bowl of hot water so that the level of water is about three-quarters of the way up the can. This will make the malt extract less viscous and easier to pour.

2) Heat about 3 litres (5 pt) of water in a large pan to around 70°C (45°F) (the exact temperature is not critical), then pour in the entire contents of the can of malt extract.

3) Stir the malt extract until it has dissolved in the hot water; this is now the wort.

If you are using liquid malt extract, it may be easier to brew a quantity of beer that allows you to use a whole can in a single brew. It is difficult to prevent malt extract from attracting wild mould spores, even if it is kept in the refrigerator.

4) Add the dried malt extract and the crushed crystal malt to the pan of wort and stir until the dried malt extract has dissolved. Bring the contents of the pan to the boil.

5) Add both types of bittering hops to the boiling wort and stir thoroughly so that they are fully soaked. Keep the wort at a rolling boil for 1 hour. Stir if necessary to ensure that the hops are well mixed into the wort.

6) Add the copper finings at the appropriate time (read the manufacturer's instructions to find out when this is).

7) Turn off the heat and allow the boiling to stop; this will only take a couple of minutes. Then stir in the aroma hops and leave them to soak for 40 minutes, stirring them into the wort a couple of times during that time.

Science stuff
The process that takes place towards the end of the boiling process is called the 'hot break'. The copper finings help protein molecules in the wort to join, forming larger molecules that precipitate from the solution. This means that the hot wort starts to clear.

8) Whilst the aroma hops are soaking, sterilize and rinse the fermenting bin.

9) Strain the wort into the fermenting bin through a large fine sieve or proprietary straining bag with the use a sterilized and rinsed jug. Take great care as the wort will still be extremely hot. <u>Do not</u> attempt to pour the hot contents of the pan directly into the sieve as you will either burn yourself or pour the wort everywhere but into the sieve.

10) Add cold tap water to bring the level in the fermenting bin to about 22 litres (4¾ gallons). Check the temperature; it should be between 18–24°C (64–75°F). Add cold tap water or boiling water to adjust the temperature accordingly and increase the volume to 25 litres (5½ gallons). If you are not able to adjust the temperature, wait until the wort has cooled to below 24°C (75°F) before moving on to the next step.

11) Adding the yeast to the fermenting bin is called 'pitching'. If you are using dried yeast, follow the manufacturer's instructions when adding it to the fermenting bin. If you have procured some brewer's yeast, mix it thoroughly with about 250 ml (9 fl oz) of wort in a sterilized and rinsed jug and then add this mixture to the fermenting bin. When you have added the yeast, rouse the wort with a large spoon or stirring rod to get as much air as possible into the beer. This will encourage the fermentation to start quickly and reduce the risk of any contamination of the wort.

If you know that a local brewery uses wet yeast, it would be well worth your while to pay them a visit and beg some yeast from them. Wet yeast improves the taste of beer and all breweries produce a lot more than they need, so they will probably be very happy to let you have some. Take along a sterilized container (you can rinse it at the brewery); you will need about 50–60 g (2 oz) for a 25-litre (5½-gallon) brew.

12) Cover the fermenting bin loosely with its lid and put it somewhere warm, preferably around 20°C (68°F). Make sure you do not cover the bin tightly with the lid because this will prevent air getting in and the yeast will not work properly. If you do not want to use the lid, make sure you put the bin somewhere that is dust- and insect-free. You can cover the bin with a clean cloth, but make sure it does not come into contact with the beer.

13) Check the specific gravity and temperature of the beer each day and record it on your brewing record sheet. When the gravity falls to around 1010 it is time to rack the beer. There will probably be a coloured band on the hydrometer indicating the specific gravity at which the beer should be racked.

14) Finings should be added to the beer to help it to clear. Some types of finings are added to the fermenting bin before the beer is racked off and others are added to the barrel or bottles; always check the manufacturer's instructions.

Follow the instruction on pages 71–3 for how to bottle and store you beer.

Tip
Keep the brewer's yeast in the fridge until you need it and then mix it with some wort before adding it to the fermenting bin. This is best done in a large, sterilized jug.

The process for making these beers is as described on pages 85–87. If the recipe recommends the use of dried malt extract, this should be added to the pan when the water is around 70°C (158°F) and stirred until it has dissolved. The grain, adjuncts and hops should be added after this.

~ IPA ~

This recipe will produce 25 litres (5½ gallons) of a full-bodied IPA with an ABV of around 5 per cent. The beer will be copper coloured with a hint of residual sweetness from the crystal malt balanced by a good hop finish from the Goldings and Northdown hops.

Extract and grain
4.5 kg (9 lb 15 oz) light dried malt extract
600 g (1 lb 5 oz) crushed crystal malt
300 g (10½ oz) flaked barley

Bittering hops
55 g (2 oz) Goldings hops
55 g (2 oz) Northdown hops

Aroma hops
15 g (½ oz) Goldings hops
15 g (½ oz) Northdown hops

~ Irish stout ~

The main characteristic of stout is a burnt bitterness, quite different from the bitterness provided by the hops, which is derived from the copious amounts of roasted unmalted barley that is included in the grain bill. This recipe makes 25 litres (5½ gallons) with an ABV of around 4 per cent.

Extract and grain
3 kg (6 lb 10 oz) premium-grade dark malt extract
500 g (1 lb 2 oz) crushed roasted barley

Bittering hops
35 g (1¼ oz) Northdown hops
10 g (⅓ oz) Galena hops

No **aroma hops** are required for this recipe.

~ Bitter ~

A bitter with a soft, malty palate, slightly hoppy and holding a thick creamy head. This recipe makes 25 litres (5½ gallons) with an ABV of around 4 per cent.

Extract and grain
3 kg (6 lb 10 oz) premium-grade pale malt extract
250 g (9 oz) crushed crystal malt

Bittering hops
50 g (2 oz) Fuggles hops
25 g (1 oz) Goldings hops

Aroma hops
35 g (1¼ oz) Styrian Goldings (or Bobek) hops

~ Best bitter ~

*This best bitter has a much more assertive hop character than the Traditional
bitter ale on pages 84–7, not just in hop bitterness but also in aroma.
This recipe makes 25 litres (5½ gallons) with an ABV of around 5.5 per cent.*

Extract and grain
3 kg (6 lb 10 oz) premium-grade pale malt extract
1 kg (2 lb 3 oz) medium dried malt extract
250 g (9 oz) crystal malt

Bittering hops
50 g (2 oz) First Gold hops
25 g (1 oz) Bramling Cross hops

Aroma hops
50 g (2 oz) East Kent Goldings hops

~ India Pale Ale ~

*These beers were originally brewed for the armed forces serving in India.
To ensure that they arrived in good condition after several weeks at sea,
they were high in alcohol and very heavily hopped. This recipe makes
25 litres (5½ gallons) of a full-bodied IPA with a good hop finish and an
ABV of around 6 per cent. It will benefit greatly from being bottled and
matured for a few months before being drunk.*

Extract and grain
4.5 kg (9 lb 15 oz) premium-grade pale malt extract
250 g (9 oz) crushed crystal malt

Bittering hops
100 g (3½ oz) Challenger hops

Aroma hops
50 g (2 oz) Cascade hops

Brewing the traditional way

Most commercial brewers make their beer from malt grain, although some smaller brewers use malt extract. As a home brewer, you can emulate the process that commercial brewers use but it does mean spending some money on the right equipment if you want to make a really good beer. There are six stages in the brewing process:

- **Mashing.** In a brewery this is carried out in the mash tun, which is the term I will use. A mash tun is an insulated vessel in which the hot liquor (the brewer's term for water) and the grist (the brewer's term for the blend of malt grains and adjuncts used to make beer) are mixed together and allowed to stand for a period of time. Each brewer will decide how long to leave the 'mash', as this mixture is called, to stand, but it is usually around 60 to 90 minutes. Because the mash tun is insulated, the temperature of the mash remains fairly constant whilst it is standing. Enzymes present in the malt work to convert the starch in the malt grain into fermentable sugars.
- **Sparging.** At the end of the mashing period, the brewer will want to extract as much of the sugars which have been produced to make the beer. After draining off the sweet malt liquor from the mash tun, the sparging process begins. Sparging involves spraying water at around 75°C (167°F) over the surface of the mash in the mash tun to wash out the remaining malt liquor.
- **Boiling.** In a brewery this is carried out in the copper, which is the term I will use. In home brewing, the copper consists of a large pan, although it is possible to use a small water boiler if you are planning to brew large quantities of beer.
- **Fermenting.** Fermenting is the process in which yeast converts the sugars present in the wort into alcohol and carbon dioxide gas.
- **Racking.** This term is used by brewers to describe the process of transferring finished beer (beer that has finished its fermentation) into barrels or bottles.
- **Conditioning.** Conditioning of the beer occurs whilst it is in the barrels or bottles. A 'secondary' fermentation occurs within the container which produces carbon dioxide gas; this gas gives the beer its sparkle or 'fizziness'.

There are two methods for brewing the traditional way; the first, called **basic all-grain brewing**, will give you very good results and the equipment cost is not as high as the second method, **advanced all-grain brewing**, although the raw material costs for the second method will be lower.

Basic all-grain brewing

Equipment for basic all-grain brewing

In addition to the equipment listed on pages 62–3 and 76, you will also need the following.

Hydrometer jar: this should be bought at the same time as the hydrometer. It is a good idea to keep it filled with fresh sterilizing solution and to keep your hydrometer in this solution, this way both the hydrometer and jar are always sterile and ready for use.

Large pan or boiler with a lid: it must be able to hold 15 litres (3¼ gallons), to use as a mash tun and copper. The pan should be made of aluminium or stainless steel and should have two robust carrying handles to make it easy and safe to empty.

Large jug: a 2-litre (3½-pt) jug is ideal. It should be made from food-grade plastic and marked with graduations so that it can be used for measuring liquid volumes. This can be bought from any home brew shop.

Additional fermenting bin: a second bin for storing the sterilizing solution is useful as you can simply wash the piece of equipment you have been using in clean, cold water and then drop it into the solution, ready for its next use.

Small watering can: is useful but not essential. This can be made from plastic or metal and should be fitted with a suitable rose which will allow you to sprinkle the hot water evenly over the surface of the mash when you are sparging. Choose a size appropriate for indoor use rather than a full size outdoor one.

Ingredients

Grist

The grist is the mixture of malted and unmalted grains, or adjuncts, which is used to make the mash. The desired constituents of the grist are decided by strength, flavour and colour of the beer.

The strength of the beer is determined by the weight of malted grains used in the grist. The flavour is decided by the combination of the flavours of each individual malt, or adjunct, used and is also affected by the hops. With experience and experimentation you'll learn what sort of flavour each type of malt brings and you'll be able to create a grist which produces a beer you really like. There are no shortcuts in home brewing; you have to brew beer, drink it, think about it and then adjust the recipe for the next brew.

The colour of the finished beer is decided by the combination of the colours of the malts and adjuncts. If you are really enthusiastic and into scientific practice, you can calculate what colour the beer will be by researching a colour measurement system based on 'Lovibond units'. This system allocates a number to each shade of colour of malt and this can be used, together with the weight of the ingredients in the grist, to calculate the finished colour 'number' of the beer. I prefer trial and error myself.

The recipe on page 96 is for a Light summer ale. The grist for this beer contains only pale malt and flaked barley. Neither of these ingredients has much colour so the finished beer will be very pale. The weight of pale malt used should produce a beer of about 4 per cent ABV. This means that the reading on the hydrometer at the start of the fermentation should be 1040; this is called the original gravity, or OG. Inexperienced home brewers may not attain an OG of 1040, so in Adjusting the weight of pale malt on page 108 I'll explain how you can change the weight of pale malt in any recipe to achieve the original gravity, and therefore the desired strength of the finished beer based on the extract from the malt you are using. The 'extract' means how much fermentable sugar you get from a specific weight of pale malt.

Types of malt

Many types of malt can be used in the production of beer.
The majority of these malts are produced from barley, although
wheat malt is used in certain beers. Refer to pages 31–4 for a detailed
breakdown of malts; I have listed some of the more popular ones below
used in this type of brewing.

Malt can be bought from home brew shops or online. If you are planning
to brew a large amount of beer and are lucky enough to live near a
maltings, you may be able to buy it directly from there. I recommend that
you buy all your ingredients in crushed form. The small additional expense
is well worth it because the people who make the malt know exactly how
much crushing to do!

Malting is a process applied to cereal grains, in which the grains are made to
germinate by soaking in water and are then quickly halted from germinating
further by drying and heating with hot air. The purpose of malting a grain is
to release enzymes, which can then be used by the brewer – you!

The malting process is very skillful and only a handful of maltings still exist.
Some are traditional in their approach whereas others utilize the latest
technology available. Here are some of the more popular grain malts used
in home brewing:

Pale malt: the basis of the majority of beer is pale malt. It provides the
beer with its main source of sugar, which the yeast converts into alcohol.
It also gives the beer a subtle flavour and golden colour.

Lager malt: a low colour, lightly modified malt for use in Pilsner and
lager beer styles.

Crystal malt: a lightly kiln-roasted malt used in recipes for its distinctive
'nutty' flavour as well as a general enriching agent in beers. It imparts the
classic 'copper' colour prevalent in bitter ales.

Chocolate malt: this is a roasted malt, which imparts colour, flavour and body to dark beers. It has a very distinctive flavour which does not appeal to everyone's palate.

Black malt: a roasted malt coloured to a higher degree than chocolate malt in the roasting process. Black malt is used to add flavour and colour in dark beers such as milds, porters and stouts.

Wheat malt: made from English wheat, wheat malt is used for its unique wheat flavour. It is much more pronounced than unmalted wheat and also has the ability to aid head formation and retention. It can also be used in the production of wheat or 'weiss' beers.

Adjuncts

Listed here are some of the more popular adjuncts used in this type of brewing; more detailed information can be found on pages 35–8.

Flaked barley: unmalted barley is steamed to soften the grain and rolled into flakes. It provides a source of unmalted starch in a readily digestible form. It gives body to light beers and adds a 'roundness' to the flavour.

Roasted barley: raw unmalted barley is roasted until it reaches its characteristic intense colour. Roasted barley imparts a 'dry' bitterness to finished beers and is often used in the production of stout. It can also be used to add colour and a distinctive flavour to bitters and strong ales.

Torrified wheat: unmalted wheat is heated until the grains 'pop' in a similar manner to popped corn. The popping process exposes the centre of the grain, which can then be used in the mash tun without any other form of pre-treatment.

Flaked maize: as with flaked barley, steam is used to soften the maize corn, which is then rolled into flakes. Used in many brewing recipes to impart a characteristic 'corny' flavour to beers.

~ Light summer ale ~

*This recipe will produce a refreshing beer that can be drunk lightly chilled
on a warm day. The pale malt gives strength and a golden colour to the beer,
whereas the flaked barley gives added body and some head retention.
The quantities listed here make 25 litres (5½ gallons) of ale with an
ABV of around 4 per cent. Remember to record the details on your
brewing record sheet (see page 117).*

Water
For the mash, you will need 10 litres (2¼ gallons) at 72° C (162°F)
For the sparge, you will need 5–10 litres (1–2¼ gallons) at 75°C (167°F)

For the grist
3.5 kg (7 lb 11 oz) crushed pale malt
70 g (2½ oz) flaked barley

Bittering hops
50 g (2 oz) East Kent Goldings hops

Aroma hops
125 g (4½ oz) East Kent Goldings hops
10 g (⅓ oz) Styrian Goldings (or Bobek) hops

You will also need
Copper finings
Packet of dried yeast large enough for 25 litres (5½ gallons)
or 50–60 g (2–2¼ oz) of brewer's yeast
Finings for the fermenting bin
Finings for the barrel or bottles

Basic all-grain brewing – mashing

Mashing, the first part of the brewing process, is a process in which the enzymes created in the malting process convert the starch in the malt into sugars, which can then ferment into alcohol. These sugars are called fermentable sugars. The solution of fermentable sugars in water is called the wort. The grist for the Light summer ale on the previous page is shown in the recipe and consists of pale malt and flaked barley.

In a brewery, the vessel used to carry out the mashing process is called a mash tun. In basic all-grain brewing you will be using a large pan to act as your mash tun. There are two crucial factors in achieving a successful mash:

- Getting the consistency of the mash right.
- Maintaining a consistent and suitable temperature of between 60–68°C (140–155°F) – the ideal temperature being 65°C (149°F) – for around 60 to 90 minutes.

1) Put 10 litres (2¼ gallons) of water into a 15-litre (3¼-gallon) pan and heat it to 72°C (162°F); check the temperature regularly with the thermometer. When the water has reached 72°C (162°F), turn off the heat.

2) Add the grist to the water using a ladle, spoon or jug and stir it gently with the stirring rod. It is important that the malt is wet, or hydrated, but do not stir the mash too much as this will release starch which may make the finished beer appear cloudy. Although the taste of the beer will not be affected, its appearance will.

3) When you have added all the grist, check the temperature of the mash – it should be between 62–68°C (144–154°F). If the temperature is too high, heat the water in the pan to a lower temperature for the next brew. If the temperature is too low, do the opposite. There will be a certain amount of trial and error to get the mash temperature correct but you will soon have perfected it. Don't forget to record the details on your brewing record sheet for future reference.

4) The mash needs to rest. Put the lid on the pan and cover it, if possible, with some form of insulation such as a cot quilt or blanket, and make sure there are no sources of ignition which may set the insulation alight. Leave the pan to stand for 75 minutes to allow the enzymes in the malt to produce the sugars that will eventually turn into alcohol. Do not be tempted to stir the mash during this time.

5) In the meantime, sterilize and then rinse a jug, sieve or straining bag and fermenting bin. The bin will be used to hold the wort prior to it going back into the pan for the next stage of brewing.

6) Place the bin on the floor as close as possible to the stove where the pan is resting. If you are using a sieve, rest it on top of the bin using the handles as supports. A good size filter bag can be suspended from the rim of the bin, allowing you to use both hands when handling the pan.

7) Use a sterilized and rinsed jug to start transferring the grain from the pan to the sieve or bag. Don't be tempted to tip the contents of the pan into the sieve or bag as most of it will probably end up either on the floor or in the fermenting bin without having gone through the sieve first. Only when you have transferred the majority of the grain into the sieve or bag can you tip the remains if you wish to.

8) While the mash is draining into the fermenting bin, rinse out the pan with cold tap water and then add about 5 litres (1 gallon) of cold tap water to the pan. Raise the temperature of the water to about 75°C (167°F) and then turn off the heat.

Basic all-grain brewing – sparging

9) To sparge the mash, wash out the jug or watering can you are planning to use for the sparging process with cold tap water. Use the jug to transfer the hot water from the pan into the watering can (if you don't have a watering can, use the water straight from the jug). Slowly pour the water evenly over the surface of the malt grain and allow it to drain into the bin. Ideally, the surface of the grain should be wetted but not flooded. Repeat this process until all the water is used up.

Sparging is a fairly time-consuming business but it is well worth the effort as it will ultimately produce more beer than if you didn't sparge. Conversely, over-sparging (using too much water during the sparging process) may extract too much starch which will make the finished beer hazy.

10) Allow the grain to drain until no more wort comes out of the sieve or bag.

11) Pour the contents of the fermenting bin back into the pan and start to bring the wort up to the boil. Leave the sieve or bag to drain into the bin whilst the wort is coming to the boil. The pan has now become the copper, which is the brewing term for the vessel that is used to boil the wort with the hops.

Basic all-grain brewing – boiling in the copper

12) Weigh out the bittering hops. Here we are using 50 g (2 oz) of East Kent Goldings, which should have an alpha acid between 5–7 per cent.

13) Add any drainings from the sieve or bag into the copper (the pan). When the wort comes to the boil, add the bittering hops and stir them in well. Keep the contents of the copper at a rolling boil for about 1 hour and stir in the hops a couple of times during the boil.

14) It is now time to add copper finings, which are used to increase the clarity of the finished beer. The most traditional form of copper finings is Irish moss, which is a type of seaweed that has been dried, called carragheen. Add the copper finings (check the manufacturer's instructions for quantities), usually about 5 minutes before the end of the boil, then turn off the heat and leave the pan to stand for 5 minutes.

15) Stir in the aroma hops and leave them to soak for about 20 minutes. At the end of the first 20 minutes, stir the hops again and leave them to soak for a further 20 minutes. The hops you add at the end of the boil do not affect the bitterness of the beer and it is not necessary to be concerned about the alpha acid content of these hops.

16) While the hops are soaking, re-sterilize the fermenting bin. Make sure you rinse the bin thoroughly before adding the wort.

17) Empty the spent grain from the sieve or bag; it makes good compost. Wash, sterilize and rinse the sieve or straining bag you used for draining the grain at the end of the mashing process and place it in position on top of the fermenting bin. Remember that the wort will still be extremely hot even though it has been standing for 40 minutes. Use the re-sterilized and rinsed jug to transfer the hopped wort into the sieve. Wear a pair of heat-resistant gloves, which will prevent your hands from getting too hot and also protect them from any splashes.

18) Empty as much out of the copper as you can and then, taking great care, pour the remaining contents of the copper through the straining device into the fermenting bin. If the copper is too heavy to handle on your own, try to get someone to assist you.

19) Add cold tap water to bring the volume of wort in the fermenting bin up to 25 litres (5½ gallons). Cover the bin with its sterilized lid and leave the contents to cool to around 20°C (68°F).

Basic all-grain brewing – pitching the yeast

20) 'Pitching' the yeast means adding the yeast to the beer. You can either use dried yeast which is available from home brew shops, or wet brewer's yeast, if you can get hold of it. If you are using dried yeast, make sure you buy a type suitable for making beer and follow the manufacturer's instructions. Whatever you do, don't use bread-making yeast! If you know that a local brewery uses wet yeast, try to get hold of some as wet yeast improves the taste of beer. Take along a sterilized container. You will need

about 50–60 g (2–2¼ oz) for a 25-litre (5½-gallon) brew. Store the brewer's yeast in the fridge until you need it and then mix it with some wort before adding it to the fermenting bin.

21) When the wort is around 20°C (68°F), add the yeast. Whether you are using dried or wet yeast it is important to give the beer a good start, so give it a good rousing with the stirring rod. Yeast needs oxygen to start working on the fermentable sugars and stirring will introduce oxygen into the beer.

Check the specific gravity of the wort with the hydrometer. It should read between 1038 and 1042 at 20°C (68°F). If the wort is not at this temperature, use the conversion chart on pages 118–9 to calculate the gravity at 20°C (68°F). You will need to know this because most hydrometers are calibrated at this temperature and the readings are only useful if they are either taken at that temperature or an adjustment is made using the table supplied.

22) Cover the fermenting bin loosely with its sterilized and rinsed lid and put it somewhere warm, preferably around 20°C (68°F) to start the fermentation process. If you are really brave, do not use the lid, just make sure that you put the bin somewhere dust- and insect-free. Do not cover the bin tightly with the lid because this will prevent air getting in and the yeast will not work properly. It is important to look after the yeast by keeping the wort at the correct temperature, between 18–24°C (64–75°F), throughout the fermentation.

23) Check the specific gravity and temperature of the beer each day and record the readings on your brewing record sheet. When the specific gravity falls to around 1010 it's time to rack the beer. There will likely be a coloured band on the hydrometer indicating the specific gravity at which the beer should be racked.

See page 73 for information on getting your beer ready to drink.

Advanced all-grain brewing

Additional equipment for advanced all-grain brewing

Suitable mash tun: Good home brew shops sell ready-made tuns which consist of a standard cool box which has been fitted with a tap, usually made of plastic. The insulated cool box allows the mashing to take place at a more or less constant temperature and the tap allows you to run off the sweet wort easily and without mess.

Water boiler: that can heat at least 30–50 litres (6½–11 gallons). The boiler will be used in the initial stages of brewing to heat water for the mash and sparge and will then convert into a copper for boiling the sweet wort and hops together.

Hop filter: which will fit into the boiler so that it can also be used as a copper. If you buy your boiler from a home brew shop, ask them to supply you with a suitable hop filter. If you buy it from somewhere else, you will have to buy a filter separately. The filter should only be used when the boiler is being used as a copper (i.e. when it has hops in it).

Although this method of brewing involves a higher initial outlay on equipment, this will be offset against the money you will save, partly by the reduced cost of the raw materials you will brew with. Malt grain is cheaper than malt extract because you are not paying someone to extract the fermentable sugars from the malt and then convert them, usually by evaporation, into a dried or liquid form which is easily transportable. More importantly, you will be able to produce some superb beers which taste as good as, if not better than, commercially produced ones.

Advanced all-grain brewing – mashing

Advanced all-grain brewing utilizes more sophisticated equipment and a different approach to mashing and sparging. This should produce better yields from your malt grain and make the brewing process less messy.

1) Heat 20 litres (4½ gallons) of water in the boiler to 72°C (162°F). Wash, sterilize and rinse the cool box mash tun.

2) Ideally, you should add the water and grist to the mash tun at the same time, which means having more than one pair of hands. You will need to seek assistance from another person to help you do this. Run about 2 litres (3.5 pt) of water at 72°C (162°F) from the boiler into the cool box mash tun.

3) Gradually add the grist while your assistant pours in another 8 litres (1¾ gallons) of water at 72°C (162°F), stirring gently all the time. Use a sterilized and rinsed jug to measure this accurately. Try to work together to produce an even mixture that has no lumps of dry malt in it. The mashing process will only work when the grist is hydrated properly; this means that all the grist must be sufficiently wetted to allow the enzymes to work effectively.

If you can't find anyone to help you, run 10 litres (2¼ gallons) of water at 72°C (162°F) from the boiler into the cool box mash tun. Use the sterilized and rinsed jug to measure the volume accurately. Add the grist, stirring gently all the time. It is important to hydrate the malt without over mixing, so add the grist slowly and stir gently. You could use a large spoon, ladle or jug to add the grist to the water.

4) You should now have ended up with a porridge-like mixture in the mash tun. Check the temperature of the mash; it should be around 65°C (149°F). The mash will need resting, so put the lid onto the mash tun and cover it with a blanket or old duvet – the more insulated it is, the better.

Mashing is a process that does not require any work, so you can leave it to stand for around 75 minutes. During this time the enzymes produced in the malting process start working on the starch in the malt and convert it into sugars. These sugars are called fermentable sugars because they will be converted into alcohol by the yeast during the fermentation process.

Do not be tempted to stir the mash, as this will increase the chances of producing excessive starch, which the enzymes will not be able to convert into sugar.

5) You now need to collect the wort. The boiler you have been using to heat up the water for the mash will soon become your copper, but at the moment it is holding hot water ready for sparging. This means that you will have to collect the wort from the mash tun in an intermediate container until the boiler is emptied. Sterilize and rinse the fermenting bin and use this to collect the wort.

Position the mash tun so that the tap is above the fermenting bin and then open the tap and allow the sweet wort to run into the bin. Let the mash drain for about 10 minutes before starting to sparge the grains; this allows some of the surface of the mash to dry slightly which will make sparging more successful.

Advanced all-grain brewing – sparging

6) Sparging is an important part of the brewing process because it will give you a better yield. Be careful not to over-sparge as this may extract too much starch which will make the finished beer hazy.

Sparging should be carried out using water at around 70–75°C (158–167°F). As a guide, use about the same amount of water for the sparge as you did for the mash (i.e. 10 litres/2¼ gallons). A small, plastic watering can or a plastic jug that has been sterilized and rinsed is a very handy device that can be used for sparging, although you can buy all sorts of fancy contraptions that will do the same job.

Sparging is not a quick process if it is done properly. Some people advise not to do it at all, but I think it is a necessary process. When sparging, ensure there is no water lying on top of the mash; allow the contents of one watering can or jug to drain through before adding the next. When you have used all the sparging water, allow the mash to drain for about 15 minutes and then close the tap. We will come back to it later.

7) The boiler will now become the copper, so drain off and discard any water left in the boiler. If you bought your boiler from a reputable home brew shop it should be supplied with a hop strainer. If you do not have one it is advisable that you get one and fit it in the boiler before you add any wort. If you don't, the tap will quickly block up with hops when you are trying to run off into your fermenting bucket.

Transfer the wort from the fermenting bin into the copper, and turn on the heat. Use the empty bin to collect any wort still in the mash tun by reopening the tap of the mash tun. You can leave the mash tun to drain whilst the wort in the copper comes to the boil.

8) When the wort comes to the boil, add the bittering hops and stir them in well. This will produce a wonderful smell. Adjust the heat to keep the contents of the copper at a rolling boil for about 1 hour. Add any wort which has drained from the mash tun to the wort in the copper.

9) Copper finings help the clarity of the finished beer. The most traditional form of copper finings is Irish moss, extracted from Carragheen, which is made from dried seaweed. You can buy copper finings from your home brew shop or online.

Add the copper finings according to the manufacturer's instructions – usually 5 minutes before then end of the boil.

10) Turn off the heat and wait for 5 minutes. Stir in the aroma hops and leave them to soak for about 20 minutes. Stir the hops again and leave them to soak for a further 20 minutes. While the hops are soaking, sterilize the fermenting bin. Make sure you rinse the bin thoroughly before adding the wort.

11) You now need to strain the hops. Open the tap on the copper and allow the hopped wort to flow into the fermenting bin. Add cold tap water to bring the volume of wort up to 25 litres (5½ gallons). Cover the bin with its sterilized lid and leave the contents to cool to around 20°C (68°F).

Adjusting hopping rates
Once you have made a beer that has a bitterness level to suit your palate, you can maintain that bitterness level by adjusting the weight of hops used according to their alpha acid content.

For instance, let's say you have created a beer that has an ideal bitterness level for your palate. On your brewing record sheet you have recorded that this particular batch of beer used 50 g (2 oz) of East Kent Goldings hops with an alpha acid of 5 per cent. But the next time you want to make the same beer, the home brew shop has Goldings hops with an alpha acid of only 4 per cent. The new weight of hops can be worked out using this formula:

New weight of hops = $\dfrac{\text{old weight} \times \text{old alpha acid}}{\text{new alpha acid}}$

In this example, the new weight = $\dfrac{50 \times 5}{4}$ = 62.5 g (2¼ oz)

This means that you would have to add 62.5 g (2¼ oz) of the new hops to achieve the same level of bitterness as with the original hops.

Adjusting the weight of pale malt

To measure the original gravity with your hydrometer, you will need to:

- Take a sample from the wort using a sterilized jug and fill the hydrometer jar, which should be placed on a level surface at a height which will allow you to read the hydrometer when it is in the jar.
- Lower the hydrometer into the wort and allow it to settle in a steady position.
- Take a reading from the hydrometer at the point where the wort is on the scale. Write down this reading – it will be around 1040.
- Remove the hydrometer and measure the temperature of the wort with a thermometer. Write down the temperature.
- Use the chart on pages 118–19 to adjust the hydrometer reading to make allowance for the temperature. If the temperature is 20°C (68°F), no adjustment is necessary.

The recipe on page 96 uses 3.5 kg (7 lb 11 oz) pale malt and should produce an OG of 1040. If the hydrometer reading shows 1035, for instance, it means that your extract (the amount of sugar produced by the malt in the mash tun) is less than you would have hoped for. This means that you will have to use more pale malt when you make this type of beer again. To calculate how much more pale malt you will need, you can use the following calculation:

New weight = $\underline{\text{original weight (in kg) x required OG}}$ (in this case it was 1040)
$\qquad\qquad\qquad$ measured OG (in this case it was 1035)

Brewers ignore the first two digits on the hydrometer reading when doing calculations, so 1040 becomes 40 and 1035 becomes 35, making the calculation as follows:

New weight = $\underline{\text{3.5 x 40}}$ = 4 kg (8 lb 13 oz)
$\qquad\qquad$ 35

Grain recipes

By the time you have reached this stage in the book you will have realized that brewing is not an exact science and is dependent on many variables such as water, malt quality and the freshness of your hop supply.

Becoming a good brewer does not happen overnight and requires much practice. It is always useful to communicate with other, ideally more experienced, brewers to develop your craft.

The taste of any beer is a very subjective issue, as with any other beverage or foodstuff. The expression 'one man's meat is another man's poison' defines how personal the like, or dislike, of a particular flavour can be.

The majority of the recipes on the following pages are based on the beers we brew at Red Rock Brewery. I have scaled down the weights of the ingredients on a pro-rata basis from our batch size of between 700–800 litres (154–176 gallons) to a 25-litre (5½-gallon) batch size. I have also changed the names of the beers to protect the innocent!

The exception is the first recipe, for which I am indebted to Hywel, who used to run the home brew shop in Plymouth, England, where I bought my initial supplies to make the trial brews for the brewery.

After brewing and tasting these beers, you may feel that you want to adjust some of the ingredients to create a beer that really suits your palate.

You can follow either the basic or the advanced all-grain brewing method to make any of the beers on the following pages.

~ Special bitter ~

This recipe will produce 25 litres (5½ gallons) of best bitter with an ABV of around 5.5 per cent. The beer will be copper coloured with a good bitter finish.

Grist
4.5 kg (9 lb 15 oz) crushed pale malt
600 g (1 lb 5 oz) crushed crystal malt
300 g (10½ oz) flaked barley

Bittering hops
100 g (3½ oz) Challenger hops

Aroma hops
35 g (1¼ oz) Goldings hops

~ Brewer's pride ~

This recipe will produce 25 litres (5½ gallons) of a full-flavoured ale with lots of character; it has an ABV of around 4.6 per cent. The three types of malt and three hop varieties give the beer a complex range of tastes.

Grist
3.4 kg (7 lb 8 oz) crushed pale malt
240 g (8½ oz) crushed amber malt
170 g (6 oz) crushed crystal malt

Bittering hops
9 g (⅓ oz) Goldings hops
10 g (⅓ oz) Northern Brewer hops
16 g (½ oz) Bobek hops

Aroma hops
26 g (1 oz) Goldings hops
12 g (⅓ oz) Northern Brewer hops
3.5 g (⅛ oz) Cascade hops

~ Hop 'n' jump ~

This recipe will produce 25 litres (5½ gallons) of a distinctive hoppy bitter with an ABV of around 4.3 per cent. In this recipe additional hops are added 10 minutes before the end of the boil. These hops contribute more to the taste and aroma than the bitterness of the beer.

Grist
3.2 kg (7 lb) crushed pale malt
220 g (8 oz) crushed amber malt

Bittering hops
12 g (⅓ oz) Cascade hops
9 g (⅓ oz) Bobek hops

Second hops (added 10 minutes before the end of the boil)
5 g (¼ oz) Cascade hops
4 g (¼ oz) Bobek hops

Aroma hops
20 g (¾ oz) Goldings hops
9 g (⅓ oz) Cascade hops
11 g (⅓ oz) Bobek hops

~ Shorten stout ~

This recipe will produce 25 litres (5½ gallons) of a full-bodied, smooth, dark beer which slips down remarkably easily. It has an ABV of around 4.5 per cent.

Grist
3.3 kg (7 lb 5 oz) crushed pale malt
200 g (7 oz) crushed crystal malt
70 g (2½ oz) crushed black malt
130 g (4½ oz) crushed roasted barley
260 g (9 oz) flaked barley

Bittering hops
6 g (¼ oz) Goldings hops
16 g (½ oz) Northern Brewer hops
5 g (¼ oz) Cascade hops

Aroma hops
7 g (¼ oz) Goldings hops
7 g (¼ oz) Northern Brewer hops
7 g (¼ oz) Cascade hops

~ Santa's delight ~

This recipe will produce 25 litres (5½ gallons) of a strong winter ale, which will warm you from the inside. If you fancy a really Christmas feel, add the optional spices with the aroma hops. They will give the beer a lovely 'nose' without overpowering the beautifully balanced malt and hop flavours.
It has an ABV of around 5.2 per cent.

Grist
3.8 kg (8 lb 6 oz) crushed pale malt
270 g (9½ oz) crushed crystal malt
230 g (8 oz) crushed amber malt
50 g (2 oz) crushed roasted barley
110 g (4 oz) flaked barley

Bittering hops
4 g (¼ oz) Goldings hops
19 g (¾ oz) Northern Brewer hops
6 g (¼ oz) Bobek hops

Aroma hops
6 g (¼ oz) Goldings hops
8 g (⅓ oz) Northern Brewer hops
13 g (½ oz) Bobek hops

Optional (but highly recommended) spices
A small piece of cinnamon stick weighing around 1 g
2–3 whole cloves
Pinch of ground nutmeg

~ Premium pale ale ~

This recipe will produce 25 litres (5½ gallons) of a full bodied pale ale with an ABV of around 4.4 per cent. There will be with a hint of colour from the crystal malt and a balanced hoppy bitterness.

Grist
3.3 kg (7 lb 5 oz) crushed pale malt
50 g (2 oz) crushed crystal malt
100 g (3½ oz) flaked barley

Bittering hops
12 g (½ oz) Goldings hops
12 g (½ oz) Fuggles hops

Aroma hops
25 g (1 oz) Goldings hops
10 g (⅓ oz) Cascade hops

~ Old fashioned mild ale ~

This recipe will produce 25 litres (5½ gallons) of mild ale with an ABV of around 3.6 per cent. Mild is a beer popular with the English working classes in the middle of the last century as it could be drunk in volume without too many side effects.

Grist
2.5 kg (5 lb 8 oz) crushed pale malt
150 g (5½ oz) crushed crystal malt
35 g (1¼ oz) crushed black malt
100 g (3½ oz) roasted barley

Bittering hops
5 g (¼ oz) Goldings hops
10 g (⅓ oz) Northern Brewer hops

Aroma hops
12 g (½ oz) Goldings hops
8 g (¼ oz) Northern Brewer hops

Brewing record sheet

It is important to keep a record the brewing process for every beer you attempt to make. This way you have an at-a-glance record of all timings and ingredients used should you wish to modify or replicate the recipe. Photocopy this template and fill it out for each brew.

Date: .... **Brew type:** ....

Grist: ....

Mash start time: .... **Mash end time:** ....

Bittering hops: ....

....

Aroma hops: ....

....

Boil start time: .... **Finings added:** ....

Boil end time: .... **Soak end time:** ....

Original gravity: .... **Temp:** ....

Day 3: Gravity: .... **Temp:** ....
Day 4: Gravity: .... **Temp:** ....
Day 5: Gravity: .... **Temp:** ....
Day 6: Gravity: .... **Temp:** ....
Day 7: Gravity: .... **Temp:** ....

Racking gravity: .... **Temp:** ....

Racking date: ....

Temp°C	15.0	15.5	16.0	16.5	17.0	17.5	18.0	18.5	19.0	19.5
Temp°F	59.0	59.9	60.8	61.7	62.6	63.5	64.4	65.3	66.2	67.1
Hydrometer Reading										
1005	-1.0	-0.9	-0.8	-0.7	-0.6	-0.5	-0.4	-0.2	-0.2	0.0
1010	-1.0	-0.9	-0.8	-0.7	-0.6	-0.5	-0.4	-0.3	-0.1	0.0
1015	-1.0	-1.0	-0.9	-0.7	-0.6	-0.5	-0.4	-0.3	-0.1	0.0
1020	-1.0	-1.0	-0.9	-0.7	-0.6	-0.5	-0.4	-0.3	-0.1	0.0
1025	-1.1	-1.0	-0.9	-0.8	-0.6	-0.5	-0.4	-0.3	-0.2	0.0
1030	-1.1	-1.0	-0.9	-0.8	-0.7	-0.5	-0.4	-0.3	-0.2	0.0
1035	-1.1	-1.0	-0.9	-0.8	-0.7	-0.5	-0.4	-0.3	-0.2	0.0
1040	-1.1	-1.0	-0.9	-0.8	-0.7	-0.6	-0.4	-0.3	-0.2	-0.1
1045	-1.1	-1.1	-0.9	-0.8	-0.7	-0.6	-0.4	-0.3	-0.2	-0.1
1050	-1.2	-1.1	-1.0	-0.8	-0.7	-0.6	-0.5	-0.3	-0.2	-0.1
1055	-1.2	-1.1	-1.0	-0.8	-0.7	-0.6	-0.5	-0.3	-0.2	-0.1
1060	-1.2	-1.1	-1.0	-0.8	-0.7	-0.6	-0.5	-0.3	-0.2	-0.1

Add or subtract the appropriate number from the grid to the reading from your hydrometer.

20.0	20.5	21.0	21.5	22.0	22.5	23.0	23.5	24.0	24.5	25.0
68.0	68.9	69.8	70.7	71.6	72.5	73.4	74.3	75.2	76.1	77.0
0.0	0.2	0.3	0.5	0.6	0.7	0.8	0.9	1.0	1.2	1.3
0.0	0.2	0.3	0.5	0.6	0.7	0.8	0.9	1.0	1.2	1.3
0.0	0.2	0.3	0.5	0.6	0.7	0.8	0.9	1.1	1.2	1.3
0.0	0.2	0.3	0.5	0.6	0.7	0.8	0.9	1.1	1.2	1.3
0.0	0.2	0.3	0.5	0.6	0.7	0.8	1.0	1.1	1.2	1.3
0.0	0.2	0.3	0.5	0.6	0.7	0.8	1.0	1.1	1.2	1.3
0.0	0.2	0.3	0.5	0.6	0.7	0.8	1.0	1.1	1.2	1.4
0.0	0.2	0.3	0.5	0.6	0.7	0.8	1.0	1.1	1.2	1.4
0.0	0.2	0.3	0.5	0.6	0.7	0.8	1.0	1.1	1.2	1.4
0.0	0.2	0.3	0.5	0.6	0.7	0.8	1.0	1.1	1.2	1.4
0.0	0.2	0.3	0.5	0.6	0.7	0.8	1.0	1.1	1.2	1.4
0.0	0.2	0.3	0.5	0.6	0.7	0.8	1.0	1.1	1.2	1.4

For instance:

**If the hydrometer reads 1035 at 16.5°C (61.7°F),
the actual reading is 1035 – 0.8 = 1034.2**

**If the hydrometer reads 1045 at 25°C (77°F),
the actual reading is 1045 + 1.4 = 1046.4**

Troubleshooting

Like most hobbies, home brewing is great when everything goes according to plan, but can be very frustrating when things go wrong. Hopefully you will not have experienced too many problems, but here are listed a number of potential problems – and solutions.

Fermentation

The beer doesn't seem to ferment at all.
- Have you added the yeast?
- Have you roused the beer properly after adding the yeast to get plenty of air into the wort?
- Is the beer too cold? If so, put it somewhere warm, such as an airing cupboard, at around 20°C (68°F).
- Was the beer too hot (over 30°C/86°F) when you added the yeast? This could have killed the yeast, so try adding another batch of yeast equivalent to the amount you used originally.

The beer started fermenting but has stopped before it is ready for racking.
- The beer may be too cold; move it somewhere warmer, such as an airing cupboard, at around 20°C (68°F).
- You may have what is known as a 'stuck fermentation'. Try rousing the beer by stirring it with a sterilized and rinsed plastic spoon or stirring rod.

The beer started fermenting but smells like rotten eggs.
- You may have covered the beer too tightly. Take the lid off the fermenting bin for a couple of hours. If the smell improves, gently rouse the beer, without introducing too much air, and cover it loosely. If the smell doesn't go away, leave the beer uncovered overnight and check it in the morning. This should improve matters

The beer is starting to clear on the surface.
- Check the specific gravity with the hydrometer; it's probably ready to be racked.

Finished beer

The beer in the barrel is flat.
- Check the manufacturer's instructions; you may have to use some sort of pressure system on the barrel.

The beer in the bottles is very lively (fizzy).
- You have either bottled the beer too soon or added too much sugar to the bottles when bottling the beer. Try chilling the bottles by placing them upright in the refrigerator for an hour or so before opening; if you prefer your beer at room temperature it will soon warm up.

The beer in the bottles is flat.
- If you have followed my advice and not added any sugar to the bottles, try moving them to a warm place, such as an airing cupboard, at around 20°C (68°F) for a week or so. Some beers, particularly stronger ones, take quite a while to condition but it will be worth waiting for.

The beer in the barrel or bottles tastes like vinegar.
- Somewhere down the line either the equipment may not have been sterilized properly or the beer has been exposed to too much air. Unfortunately you'll have to write this one off to experience as there is no remedy for vinegary beer.

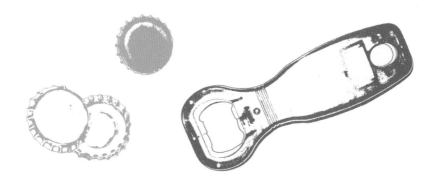

ABV: alcohol by volume. The amount of alcohol present in the beer by percentage volume. A beer with an ABV of 5 per cent contains 5 ml of alcohol per 100 ml of beer.

adjunct: any grain added to the grist which has not been derived from malted barley.

alpha acids: these are the constituent of hops that add bitterness to beer.

attenuation: a measure of how much of the fermentable sugar in the original wort has been converted into alcohol.

barley: a cereal grain which is converted into malt by the process of malting.

bittering hops: hops that are added to the *copper* at the start of the boil. These hops add bitterness due to their alpha acid content, but little or no aroma.

Burton Union sets: a row of fermentation casks with overflows that allow the excess yeast produced in the fermentation to flow into a common trough, allowing the overflow to be recirculated into the casks.

copper: the vessel used to boil the sweet wort from the mash tun with hops.

copper finings: finings that are added to the copper to aid the coagulation of proteins present in the wort. These help the finished beer to clear more easily.

diastatic power (DP): the ability of the enzymes in a grain to convert starch into fermentable sugars.

diastatic malt extract (DME): malt extract in a concentrated liquid form.

fermenting bin: vessel that holds the beer during the fermentation process.

finings: used in several stages of the production of beer; they aid the clarification of the finished beer. Apart from copper finings there are primary and secondary finings which are used either in the fermentation bin or the finished beer container (i.e. barrels or bottles).

grist: the blend of malt grains and adjuncts used to make the mash.

hops: hops give bitterness, flavour and aroma to beer. The time of addition to the copper will determine which of these roles the hops will play.

hydrometer: a device for measuring the specific gravity of the wort or beer. The strength of a beer can also be determined using measurements from a hydrometer.

lagering: the process of storing beer, generally bottom-fermenting lager style beers, at a low temperature for a period of time to allow the beer to mature.

lambic: a beer which is produced by spontaneous fermentation involving wild yeast. It has a distinctive flavour.

liquor: a name given by brewers to the water used in the brewing process.

malt: in its original form, malt is a whole grain which has been converted from barley by the process of malting.

malt extract: is available in liquid (syrup) or dried (powdered) form. It is produced by concentrating the wort produced in the mashing process and contains fermentable sugars ready for the brewing process.

maltings: a place where barley is converted into malt grain.

mash: a mixture of the grist and hot liquor used to produce the sweet wort which eventually ferments to create beer.

mashing: a process that takes place in the mash tun when enzymes present in the malt grain convert the starch in the mash into sugar-producing wort.

mash tun: the vessel in which the mash is mixed and stood whilst the mashing process takes place.

microbrewery: a small-scale brewery which generally produces a range of beers often in casks and sometimes in bottles.

noble hop: the term traditionally refers to four central European varieties of hop: Hallertau, Tettnanger, Spalt and Saaz.

pilsner: sometimes called pilsener or pils, is a pale lager beer developed in the 19th century in a town called Pilsen in the Czech Republic.

racking: separating the finished beer from the unwanted solids which are left on the bottom of the fermenting bin at the end of the fermentation.

starch: a polysaccharide carbohydrate present in barley which is converted into fermentable saccharides (sugars) during the malting and mashing processes.

sparging: spraying or running water at around 75°C (167°F) over the finished mash to extract sugars from the grain.

tannin: is extracted, along with alpha acids, from hops in the copper. Generally, they are not a desired addition to beer because of their astringent nature.

wort: the sweet malt sugar solution which is produced in the mash tun and then boiled with hops to produce the liquid which will be fermented into beer.

References

Charles Faram & Co Ltd: www.wellhopped.co.uk

John Parkes: john@redrockbrewery.co.uk

Tuckers Maltings: www.tuckersmaltings.co.uk

Warminster Maltings: www.warminster-malt.co.uk

Wikipedia: www.wikipedia.org

Yakima Chief Ranches: www.yakimachief.com/hopvarieties

Suppliers

UNITED KINGDOM
Charles Faram & Co Ltd
The Hopstore
Monksfield Lane
Newland
Nr Malvern
Worcester WR13 5BB
www.charlesfaram.co.uk

Hop Shop
22 Dale Road
Mutley
Plymouth
Devon PL4 6PE
www.hopshopuk.com

Palmers Brewery
The Old Brewery
West Bay Road
Bridport
Dorset DT6 4JA
www.palmersbrewery.com

Tuckers Maltings
Teign Road
Newton Abbot
Devon TQ12 4AA
www.tuckersmaltings.co.uk

NEW ZEALAND
Aqua-Vitae
268 Lincoln Rd
Addington
Christchurch
www.aquavitae.co.nz

Brewcraft
19 Mt Eden Road
Mt Eden
Auckland
store.mteden@brewcraft.co.nz

UNITED STATES
Home Sweet Homebrew
2008 Sansom Street
Philadelphia, PA 19103
www.homesweethomebrew.com

Karp's Homebrew Shop
2 Larkfield Road
East Northport, NY 11731
www.homebrewshop.com

The Weekend Brewer
4205 West Hundred Road
Chester, VA 23831
www.weekendbrewer.com